Maserati
250F

A TECHNICAL APPRAISAL

Maserati
250F

A TECHNICAL APPRAISAL

ANDY HALL

Foulis

Haynes

A **FOULIS** MOTORING BOOK

First Published 1990

© RACECAR ENGINEERING 1990

Published by:
Haynes Publishing Group
Sparkford, Near Yeovil, Somerset BA22 7JJ
England

Haynes Publications Inc.
861 Lawrence Drive, Newbury Park,
California, 91320, USA

Produced for GT Foulis & Co. by
RACECAR ENGINEERING
(Racecar Engineering Specialist Publications)
Telephone or Fax (0935) 31295
Editorial Director: Ian Bamsey
Research Assistant: Alan Lis

British Library Cataloguing in Publication
Data
Hall, Andy
Maserati 250F - a technical appraisal
1. Racing cars
I. Title
629.2222

ISBN 0-85429-803-7

Library of Congress Catalog
Card number 90-83290

Printed in England by:
J. H. Haynes & Co. Ltd.
Typesetting & Artwork by:
Photosetting, Yeovil, Somerset

INTRODUCTION

Technically speaking, the Maserati 250F was a very ordinary motor car for the business of Grand Prix racing. It broke no new ground, inspired no path of fresh development. Indeed, it was one of the last of the historic front engined cars, dinosaurs awaiting sudden death.

The 2.5 litre dinosaurs roamed from 1954 until 1957: big, heavy brutes slurping alcohol and sliding around on low grip tyres. Within a few short years the Grand Prix car was a small, light petrol-sipping projectile with a mid engine and high grip tyres. The dinosaurs were in museums.

Somehow the 250F embodied the spirit of the brutally exciting era that ended so abruptly after Fangio won his fifth and final World Championship in 1957. Perhaps because Fangio won that title in a 250F. Perhaps because the 250F flourished throughout the years of 2.5 litres and free fuel, often the most popular model on the grid.

More likely because of its sheer charisma. Although uninspired in the technical sense, it embodied everything a Grand Prix car stood for in the days when racing drivers rode on rather than in the car. More than that, it was the car in which Fangio perfected the exhilarating technique of four wheel drift.

Although a cherished classic rather than a technical triumph, the 250F makes a fascinating engineering study. It didn't shine in any one particular area but it did everything rather well, hence its long competitive life. Indeed, it survived throughout the four year formula for which it was devised without falling from grace.

The cars of this period were far from lumbering dinosaurs. In studying the technology of the Maserati 250F we can appreciate the raw beauty of the last era of innocence before scientific progress swept aside the romantic notion of the Grand Prix car as a war horse ridden by a hero.

All photographs are from the archives of London Art Tech (LAT), Standard House, Bonhill Street, London EC2A 4DA.

BACKGROUND

Breathe Deeply

Grand Prix engine development took a major turn in the early Fifties with fall of forced induction but chassis technology remained static. Thus, the pattern of early Fifties Grand Prix chassis design was that set before the war, in the heady days when Daimler-Benz and Auto Union spent vast sums on racing development. A good proportion of that went into supercharged engine development but later rule makers left that a blind alley. Thus, the legacy of the German giants was the classic post-Vintage front engined racing car chassis.

Theirs had been an affluent, science-led period in the Thirties, prior to which the Grand Prix car had been an unsophisticated device with a flimsy ladder frame girder chassis running on heavy, crude leaf spring suspended beam axles. The German companies formulated the concept of a torsionally rigid tubular chassis with a low centre of gravity carrying suspension designed for proper control of wheel movement over bumps and while cornering. At least, that was the theory behind their endeavours. In practice torsional rigidity and wheel control were still far from perfect in the late Thirties.

The new breed of scientific car had independence of wheel movement, at least at the front and was clothed in a streamlined light alloy body that concealed even the radiator. Auto Union's example pioneered twin leading shoe brakes and the use of the ZF limited slip differential but its strange mid engine layout was not a trendsetter. A combination of trailing arm front and swing axle rear suspension may well have been the root of off-putting handling difficulties. Meanwhile, Daimler-Benz improved the traditional front engined layout, exploiting the de Dion rear axle together with independent front suspension via parallel, unequal wishbones and coil-springs.

The de Dion system employed a transverse tube which was pivoted at its centre-point with the pivot allowed to rise and fall in a vertical slot. Thus, no lateral movement was permitted while radius arms running back to the hubs from the chassis side rails prevented fore and aft movement. Consequently the hubs were free only to rise and fall, the effect of the tube being to keep the wheels parallel at all times. Since each radius arm worked through an arc this had the effect of trying to twist the transverse tube so provision was made for rotation of outer sections of the tube relative to its centre section.

The long known, rediscovered de Dion system provided for a low roll centre and with the rear tyres kept parallel and perpendicular to the track surface good grip and handling could be achieved. A stable understeer characteristic was shown by Daimler Benz to be attainable for a front engined car having a combination of reasonably stiff frame, de Dion rear axle and independent front suspension. The de Dion-controlled rear wheels had to be driven by universally-jointed half shafts from a chassis mounted final drive which could be set in unit with the gearbox. In '37 Daimler Benz produced a compact transverse gearbox to maximise the potential of this layout for good weight distribution.

Earlier, in 1933 the Italian Maserati brothers had pioneered hydraulic brake activation (though a water-filled system had been employed by Murphy's famous 1921 French Grand Prix winning Duesenberg) and this technology had been adopted by Daimler Benz and Auto Union. In turn inspired by the Germans, the Maserati family had first tried independent front suspension in 1935 and they took this over to Indianapolis while the richer Daimler Benz and Auto Union teams dominated Grand Prix events.

Four car-obsessed Maserati brothers - Alfieri, Bindo, Ettore and Ernesto - had been involved in international motor racing under their family name and the Trident of Bologna since 1926. By 1930 they had established themselves as a serious force in Grand Prix racing, challenging Bugatti. Alfieri sadly died in 1932, the survivors fought on. Further glory was won against the Scuderia Ferrari Alfa Romeo team but the Maserati family concern could not hope to compete squarely with those giants that subsequently emerged north of the Alps.

Consequently, at Bologna in the late Thirties the emphasis was on 1.5 litre "Voiturette" racing. The exception was Indianapolis, a privately entered, supercharged 3.0 litre 8CTF Grand Prix model Maserati winning the 1939 and 1940 500 mile classics. Maserati had a policy of selling its straightforward racing designs to private entrants - hence its keen interest in the popular Voiturette category - and the Indianapolis project arose through customer demand.

In traditional style the 8CTF had a ladder frame chassis with a beam-type rear axle suspended on quarter-elliptic springs. However, the frame was composed of deep box section welded steel and magnesium side and cross-members with one of the cross-members forming the oil tank. The front suspension was fully independent with a rocker arm for each wheel operating a torsion bar. The gearbox was in unit with the eight cylinder supercharged engine while a torque tube drive to the rear axle fed via a spur gear assembly on the nose of the axle. A low drive helped keep the engine and gearbox and the driving position low, hence the centre of gravity was low.

Although less advanced than the rival 3.0 litre German Grand Prix cars, the 8CTF was sophisticated by Brickyard standards. Its chassis was a step ahead of contemporary American cars in terms of rigidity, wheel control and braking. Huge, hydraulically operated 16" diameter magnesium drum brakes provided real braking: drifting into the sweeping turns was the order of the day given the mechanical brakes in regular use.

Blown via twin Roots-type blowers and drinking 80% methanol, the Maserati straight eight engine produced a respectable 350b.h.p. at 6,500r.p.m. Roots rather than the usual centrifugal-type Indy Car blowers provided higher boost coming off the turns, the 8CTF could out-brake and out-handle the Indy Car opposition and Wilbur Shaw took comfortable wins. He was leading again in 1941 when a wheel collapsed, dashing his hopes of a hat-trick.

The 8CTF was the first of the Viale Ciro Menotti, Modena produced Maserati single seaters. Early in 1938 the Italian industrialist Commendatore Adolfo Orsi had acquired the Officine Alfieri Maserati SpA, moving it from its traditional Bologna home and installing his son Omer as Managing Director. The three surviving Maserati brothers entered into a service agreement which kept them with the company until 1947.

Although primarily interested in Maserati's general engineering interests, the Orsi family saw valuable prestige in motor racing. For 1939 all Italian races were confined to 1.5 litres and Maserati responded with an important new Voiturette, the 4CL. Its chassis broadly followed 8CTF practice while its new in line four engine was "square" rather than markedly under-square as the straight eight and earlier fours had been. Innovatively, it boasted twin overhead camshafts and four valves per cylinder at an included angle of 90 degrees. A single blower helped extract 220b.h.p. (146.7 b.h.p per litre compared to 116.7 for the 8CTF) at 6,600r.p.m.

The first outing for the 4CL as a works car was the 1939 Tripoli Grand Prix, for which Daimler-Benz built a scaled down version of its state-of-the-art Grand Prix car. The Tripoli circuit was extremely fast and Maserati tried a streamlined fully enveloping body which helped Luigi Villoresi secure pole position. Alas, all three works entries retired on the first lap. Nevertheless, a number of lesser races fell to the 4CL before war intervened.

Alfa Romeo had meanwhile strengthened its rival straight eight Type 158 with two stage supercharging and had reached 254b.h.p. (169.3b.h.p. per litre) at 7,600r.p.m. The 158 had a tubular frame, trailing link independent front suspension, swing axle independent rear suspension and its gearbox in unit with the differential. It was a sophisticated car and when, in 1947, Grand Prix racing resumed to a formula of 1.5 litres supercharged or 4.5 litres unsupercharged, the 158 was the class of the field. Supercharging and fuel developments saw power soar towards 300b.h.p.

In 1948 Maserati replied with the 4CLT/48, the first new model to appear following the departure of the Maserati brothers, who went on to form the Osca concern. Nevertheless, a number of its innovations had been evaluated under the brothers. Two stage supercharging was one such, and with the higher boost thus obtained power rose to 260b.h.p. at 7,000r.p.m. Otherwise the engine was familiar while the chassis was new, and of tubular construction (hence the T designation) with two parallel 100mm. diameter side rails linked by various cross members. It carried independent front suspension via wishbones and coil springs while retaining a leaf spring suspended rigid rear axle. Reduction gears on the nose of the differential unit lowered the propeller shaft for a low driving and engine position.

Although Maserati now employed a tubular frame, this was still essentially of the classic ladder pattern. In contrast, the Cisitalia car designed by Porsche at this time pioneered a "spaceframe" approach to chassis construction. Porsche employed a well triangulated multi tubular frame which was significantly more rigid, particularly in torsion. A pure spaceframe in which all tubes are arranged so as to be free from bending loads was an impossible ideal given the need to provide a cockpit opening but a well triangulated multi tubular frame could provide a high level of stiffness, as Porsche appreciated. Alas, the exciting Cisitalia project went bankrupt.

While a stiff chassis frame was a goal for which Auto Union designer Porsche and his rivals at Daimler Benz had striven before the war, it was only desirable given proper exploitation of fully independent suspension. The move by Daimler Benz to a de Dion rear axle was indicative of the difficulties facing a designer striving for uncompromised wheel control. Further, low tyre grip limited cornering potential: around 0.75 g was the maximum lateral acceleration it was possible to obtain at this time. In the light of these considerations the general approach of the austere early post war years was that of hard springs and a somewhat flexible frame - the Vintage recipe. However, the high unsprung weight of the beam axle had been shed with the advent of front wishbones and a non structural de Dion tube at the rear.

The 4CLT/48 was an improvement over the 4CL but Alfa Romeo made a comparable step through general development work and the differential between the rival Italian marques remained. Alfa Romeo withdrew in '49 but Ferrari's improving 1.5 litre V12 supercharged car designed by Type 158 creator Gioacchino Colombo was by then ready to assume its mantle. Using two stage Roots supercharging Ferrari obtained 2.4 bar absolute and at 7,800r.p.m. power was 315b.h.p. Alfa Romeo reasserted itself in 1950 - reaching 350b.h.p. as boost and revs rose - then '51 brought a titanic struggle between the super-boosted 1.5 litre supercharged Alfa Romeo and a new 4.5 litre unblown Ferrari.

The supercharged Grand Prix engine had been relentlessly developed since the Twenties. Come the Fifties and the state-of-the-art two-stage forced induction device fielded by Alfa Romeo was capable of almost 240b.h.p per litre, relying heavily on engine speed and boost for its performance. In terms of power per litre per 1000r.p.m. per bar boost there was no significant improvement over the German cars of the Thirties. Running high boost the supercharged engine was highly sensitive to tuning, fuel, even atmospheric conditions. Fuel consumption was high, as were internal stresses and it is reported that the Alfa Romeo Type 158 crankshaft had to be replaced every few races.

It was in the light of the enormous expense involved that Ferrari had turned to the 4.5 litre unblown alternative option, having then to find 80b.h.p. per litre to be competitive. Colombo had left Maranello and his replacement Aurelio Lampredi eagerly pursued this route since the marque's unsupercharged 2.0 litre Formula Two car already comfortably achieved that figure. In 1951 a 4.5 litre V12 Ferrari vanquished Alfa Romeo at Silverstone, vindicating the normally aspirated choice.

In the meantime the Maserati four cylinder engine had lost reliability with increasing supercharging pressure and, reluctant to go to the expense of an all new high boost power plant, or to grasp the nettle of the unknown 4.5 litre alternative, the marque had faded once more from the forefront of Grand Prix racing. Omer Orsi turned his attention instead to Formula Two, the category replacing the pre-war Voiturette cars and catering solely for unsupercharged 2.0 litre single seaters.

A new 2.0 litre car was developed for the '52 season when lack of interest in Grand Prix racing following the withdrawal once again of Alfa Romeo saw rounds of the new Drivers' Championship held to Formula Two regulations. This situation was to continue until 1954, when a new Formula One category was ushered in, this catering for 2.5 litre unsupercharged cars, with a forced induction option of just 750cc. In the early Fifties the spotlight swung firmly back upon unblown engines.

Giving normally aspirated engines over three times the displacement of a supercharged rival was perhaps fair in terms of equating maximum power outputs at the time the formula was determined but it was clear that the atmospheric engine had a lot more development potential. Further, for a given power level the smaller supercharged engine would be more heavily stressed and could therefore be expected to be less reliable while its inevitable use of excess fuel as an internal coolant implied a higher fuel consumption. Worse, as engine speed rose in pursuit of power, the supercharged engine needed a centrifugal-type rather than Roots-type blower at the expense of the shape of its power curve.

This much had been demonstrated by the supercharged V16 BRM which had extracted 500b.h.p. from 1500cc by running heavily pressurised - over 5.0 bar - to a five figure engine speed. That feat showed that a 750cc. engine could be coaxed to give 250b.h.p. matching the 100b.h.p. per litre performance anticipated from the forthcoming 2.5 litre engines. However, with its very high engine speed and its centrifugal blowers the BRM had a very narrow power curve together with dubious reliability and excessive thirst. By the early Fifties it was clear that 100b.h.p. per litre was within the grasp of a more civilised atmospheric racing car engine, matching the performance of contemporary racing motorcycles, though Formula Two cars had yet to see an honest 200b.h.p.

Prior to the entry of Maserati, Formula Two was contested primarily by Ferrari, Simca-Gordini and Alta-H.W.M. Ferrari had been active in Formula Two since 1947 and by 1950 had developed a highly competitive V12 machine with a tubular steel frame (based on oval-section side members and having a stiffening scuttle framework). The Ferrari front suspension was somewhat crude employing a transverse leaf spring together with double wishbones but its version of the de Dion rear axle broke new ground.

Ferrari Formula Two designer Lampredi had introduced a new fore-and-aft location for the de Dion tube via two parallel radius rods each side which allowed the hubs to rise and fall without imparting a twisting force. Dispensing with the rotating joints left the tube lighter and Lampredi located the sliding vertical guide for it ahead of the final drive unit. This beneficially shifted weight forwards, reducing the moment of polar interia. That reduction of the 'dumb bell effect' made the car more responsive to steering input.

As at the front, Lampredi's suspension medium was a single transverse leaf spring and as usual Houdaille rotary vane-type shock absorbers were employed. A four speed transverse gearbox was in unit with the differential which fed through universally-jointed half shafts. A ZF limited slip differential was employed, as was a conventional multi-plate clutch. Braking was by 13.8 inch diameter light alloy drums with twin leading shoes, hydraulically activated.

With its 80b.h.p. per litre the well developed Ferrari V12 engine was powerful by Formula Two standards but Lampredi favoured development of a lighter, more compact four cylinder engine intended to offer a broader power band. The rival four cylinder Alta engine gave only 140b.h.p. compared to 160b.h.p. for the Maranello V12 yet the light, nimble H.W.M. could hustle the Ferrari on circuits where there was a premium upon acceleration and sheer 'driveability'.

The Alta engine, it should be noted, produced neither greater power nor greater torque than the Ferrari V12. Torque, essentially, is the turning force produced on the crankshaft by combustion pressure on the pistons and the power required to propel a car at any given speed is a product of torque - the work done - and crankshaft speed - the rate at which the work is done. The Ferrari V12 was designed to operate at a relatively high crankshaft speed compared to the lower power Alta engine. Ferrari saw 7500r.p.m. as its peak power speed, Alta only 6,500r.p.m.

The weaker Alta engine boasted a comparable level of torque and, significantly, useful power over a wider range of engine operating speed, hence its delivery of superior low speed performance and its excellent driveability. Lampredi reasoned that the peak power speed - hence the power - reached by the V12 could be matched by a carefully designed brand new four cylinder engine with the benefit of useable power over a significantly broader range of operating speed.

Theoretically, there is no reason why a four cylinder engine should give a broader range of power than a twelve cylinder engine of the same displacement given a similar peak power speed. Where then, did Lampredi see an advantage? He appreciated that the key to the performance of the Alta engine was its excellent breathing and he wanted to explore the same route. This followed the approach pioneered by the contemporary unsupercharged Norton motorcycle racing engine which produced 100b.h.p. per litre.

While car racing engineers had been exploring the vast potential of supercharging, Norton had given careful attention to gas flow and combustion in an atmospheric engine. Of particular importance was the inlet porting, the branched manifold feed from a conventional shared carburettor causing a significant loss of volumetric efficiency compared to the straighter run from atmosphere to port allowed by individual carburettors. Norton had shown that such a free-breathing inlet system, either sidedraught or downdraught, could be gainfully employed in conjunction with carefully dimensioned inlet stacks exploiting pressure wave tuning principles.

In essence, it was possible to harness the energy present in the pressure waves that travel up and down the inlet pipe to assist breathing. Resonance in the pipe could cram more air into the engine at a given operating speed. That speed was determined by the length of the pipe:

altering its length varied the engine speed at which it would resonate to the benefit of cylinder filling. Clearly, the power band could be widened by tuning the inlet system to enhance cylinder filling at a speed some way below the peak power speed. With a V12 engine it was extremely difficult to arrange for individual carburettors and tuned inlet stacks. Thus, for logistical reasons Lampredi moved to four cylinders.

That focused attention upon engine stress. The far larger cylinders implied a greater reciprocating mass and a longer stroke, hence higher piston speeds. Seeking high engine speed, Lampredi plumped for over-square dimensions of 90mm. x 78mm. (a stroke:bore ratio of 0.87:1) compared to the virtually square dimensions of 60mm. x 58.8mm. for the V12 (a stroke:bore ratio of 0.98). The effect was to increase the mean piston speed at 7500r.p.m. from a very modest 2882 feet per minute to 3822 feet per minute. That was a figure still within the limits considered acceptable at this time. Had Lampredi retained the stroke:bore ratio of the V12 he would have run well into the region above 4000 feet per minute which was considered hazardous.

A conventional hemispherical head was accessed via twin overhead camshaft controlled valves, two per cylinder at an included angle of 58 degrees. The piston was domed to achieve the desired 12.0:1 compression ratio which was made possible through the use of high octane fuel, though not the exotic mixes used by rivals. The porting followed the Alta pattern and ignition was via two plugs per cylinder to assist combustion. Thanks to better breathing and better burning there was a marked increase in combustion efficiency over the earlier single cam, single plug V12.

This 1951 engine's hallmark was sophistication: a fresh approach in the motor racing world after years of chasing power through the brute force of high boost and trick fuel. Indeed, this engine was designed to run on a mild 20:80 alcohol: petrol mix in the interest of completing a race without refuelling (Formula Two events running over shorter distances than Grands Prix). Nevertheless, running to 7,500r.p.m. the new four cylinder Ferrari engine produced 170b.h.p. with little development work while peak torque was achieved at a shade under 5,000r.p.m. and the power curve was satisfyingly fatter. The net result was a much broader, much more useful power band while the weight saving was the best part of 25% over the V12 lump.

Lampredi's more efficient in line four featured hairpin valve springs and was based on a deep alloy crankcase that carried the crankshaft on five rather than the more typical three plain bearings. A gear train off the nose of the crankshaft drove the camshafts and also the water and oil pumps and the twin magnetos required for the dual ignition. The head was cast integrally with the alloy block and wet steel liners were screwed into recesses formed around the combustion chambers. The liners were sealed at the bottom by rubber O-rings. Much attention was paid to internal cooling since the engine was designed to run on such a low alcohol fuel in the interest of good consumption.

The Lampredi four emerged for bench tests in the spring of 1951 and contested the Modena Grand Prix at the end of the season, showing a marked superiority over the successful V12 unit. For 1952 the four cylinder car was the mainstay of the Ferrari programme and was crushingly successful. Only once was it beaten, the under-financed straight six Gordini triumphing on home soil at Rheims. However, the new straight six Maserati was the moral victor of the Modena Grand Prix right at the end of the season.

The six cylinder A6G Maserati was the work of Antonio Bellentani and Alberto Massimino. Like the Gordini it had the square cylinder dimensions of 75mm. x 75mm, the over square racing engine as yet a rarity. The engine had been derived from a sports car six designed by the Maserati brothers. However, that under-square sports car engine had been based on an iron block and had employed a single overhead camshaft whereas the new generation bigger bore, shorter stroke power plant had an aluminium block and a redesigned head with twin overhead camshafts, though still only two valves per cylinder.

The dry sump Formula Two engine was all alloy with a detachable head and its smaller bore made for an inherently more compact combustion chamber than enjoyed by the Ferrari four. A single plug was employed. With smaller pistons and a shorter stroke Maserati could run to a higher speed for a given level of stress but did not plan to venture much beyond 7000r.p.m. Significantly higher speed would have brought with it breathing difficulties and a lower quality of ignition. Magneto ignition was almost universal at this time. A magneto is a form of permanent-magnet alternating-current generator driven directly by the engine and providing ignition energy without the need for a battery. It is limited in its ability to provide for multi cylinder engines at high speed.

The crankcase split at the level of the crank axis to provide positive support for the crankshaft from above and below in traditional Maserati fashion. The steel crankshaft ran in seven plain Vandervell thinwall bearings and as a consequence the cylinders were widely spaced. Cast iron dry liners, flanged at the top, were carried by a block which was of closed deck construction. Conventional aluminium pistons drove nickel-chrome I-section steel con rods, these replacing the Maserati's traditional tubular items.

The aluminium alloy pistons were of the solid skirt type with four rings, a second oil control ring set below the gudgeon pin. The combustion chamber was hemispherical while the valve angle was 90 degrees included and valve operation was via finger cam followers avoiding side thrust on the valve stem. Two coil springs closed each valve. The twin overhead camshafts each ran in four bearings and were gear driven from the nose of the crankshaft. The gear train also drove the oil and water pumps and the magneto.

Three rather than six carburettors were employed: twin choke Weber 38 DCOs, thus each cylinder had its own inlet passage. With only single ignition the 14mm. plug was central in the combustion chamber. Two three branch exhaust manifolds were standard. With development, the Maserati six - longer and heavier than Lampredi's four - was coaxed to give a healthy 165b.h.p. at 7,000r.p.m. running a 13:1 compression ratio and a very strong brew to match. Overall, however, it must be considered a less efficient unit than the more successful Maranello four.

Since a sidedraught straight six is wide on the induction side the engine was offset slightly in a new chassis frame. The gearbox - offering four speeds - was in unit with the engine then a long prop shaft ran back at an angle to the final drive, which was in the centre of a rigid rear axle. Again spur reduction gears lowered the prop shaft while the axle was suspended on quarter-elliptic springs and was also connected to the chassis via parallel tubular radius rods. Houdaille rotary vane-type dampers and an anti roll bar were standard equipment front and rear, and again the front suspension was via unequal-length parallel wishbones and coil springs. This form of linkage kept the outer front tyre upright while cornering, albeit imparting some unwanted positive camber to the inner wheel.

The Maserati brakes were 13.4" inch diameter light alloy drums worked by twin leading shoes with shrunk-in ferrous linings. Steering was via worm and sector box. The chassis frame was a chrome-molybdenum tubular structure similar to that of the 4CLT/48, with 80mm. diameter side rails. The fuel tank was mounted in the tail and it formed part of the body with the oil tank bolted to the back of it under a small tail-piece cowl. The body shape resembled that of the four cylinder car and was designed to clothe the mechanicals in a manner assumed to be conducive to good airflow. However, the new machine was slightly lower, with a lower driving position, this for a smaller frontal area hence less drag and it had a longer snout. Dry weight was quoted as a mere 500kg.

The prototype A6G made its debut in South America early in 1952 driven by Nello Pagani and disappointing performances at Rio de Janeiro and Buenos Aires saw the European debut held over until June 8 and the 'Autodrome Grand Prix' at Monza. For this race Maserati entered the strong team of Juan Manuel Fangio, Josc Froilan Gonzalez and Felice Bonetto. World Champion Fangio had raced the BRM V16 in Ireland the previous day and had then driven down from Paris. He arrived tired and too late to practice. Following the withdrawal of Alfa Romeo Fangio was freelancing and this weekend he was trying to do too much: uncharacteristically he crashed at Lesmo on the second lap. He injured a joint in his neck and was out for the rest of the season, this blow greatly weakening the 1952 Maserati challenge.

The Monza race was a two heat affair: Gonzalez

retired from heat one with magneto trouble while Bonetto finished fourth. In the second heat Bonetto was holding third when his fuel pump failed not far from the finish. He pushed in to claim ninth place, seventh on aggregate. Bonetto was Maserati's only driver on the next works outing for the A6G, in the German Grand Prix at the Nurburgring on August 3. He qualified indifferently, spun on the first lap and suffered tyre failure. He made it back to the pits, then completed his second lap nonchalantly smoking a pipe! Disqualification followed.

For the Italian Grand Prix at Monza on September 7 Maserati had a new twin plug version of the six cylinder engine developing almost 180b.h.p. at 7000r.p.m. The second magneto was driven off the exhaust cam. The works team was back to three cars, Gonzalez rejoining Bonetto while Franco Rol took the third seat. The policy was to try to build a strong lead then refuel without losing it, since the frugal Ferraris would run non-stop. Full, a 200 litre tank weighed around 80kg.

Starting with a part load, Gonzalez got 20 seconds ahead of Alberto Ascari, but it wasn't enough and he finished just over a minute behind in second place. Bonetto was fifth while Rol retired. A week later at Modena Ascari retired and Gonzalez finished on the tail of Luigi Villoresi's Ferrari after a bad piece of baulking cost him the lead. Only one other works car had been entered, for Bonetto, and it had non-started due to a failed radiator core plug as it was driven down from the factory.

So it was that the '52 season at least ended on a high note, in spite of the loss of Fangio. For 1953 the Great Colombo strengthened the Maserati technical staff and the A6G was heavily revised as the A6SSG, whereas the rival Ferrari remained essentially unchanged, aside from an included valve angle of 100 degrees for further improved breathing together with a lower engine profile. Changes to the Maserati engine in the wake of Colombo's arrival were far more extensive.

The cylinder dimensions were revised to a distinctly over square 76.2mm. x 72mm. in a quest for more valve area and higher revs - up to 8000r.p.m. with a margin of safety. The '52 engine saw a mean piston speed of 3431 feet per minute at 7000r.p.m. and that would have risen to 3921 feet per minute had it run to 8000r.p.m. whereas the revised engine saw a more comfortable 3764 feet per minute at its 8000r.p.m. peak power speed. At the same time the increase in valve area assisted breathing at high speed.

With the bigger bore came a 77 degree included valve angle and thus a more compact combustion chamber for which Colombo fashioned a revised shape to suit the twin plug ignition and the high compression ratio necessary to get the most out of the potent fuel that was permitted. This clever design was a derivative of the pent roof type with squish areas either side on the longitudinal axis, on which was also the plug location. The plugs were situated one each side of the roof line in between the two squish areas, the longitudinal cross section resembling that of a Bowler hat.

The squish area displaced mixture in the direction of the plug, promoting turbulence which is conducive to good combustion while helping 'fan the flames' to the same end. The compression ratio went to 13.75:1, bigger Weber 40 DCO3 twin choke carburettors were fitted and the power output increased to 190b.h.p. at 8000r.p.m. That represents 95b.h.p. per litre and 11.875b.h.p. per litre per 1000r.p.m.

Modifications to the chassis were just as extensive, with a stronger scuttle stiffening superstructure and a sleeker body, the latter clearly influenced by Ferrari styling. Streamlining was an art not a science these days. The suspension was refined, the fuel tank was enlarged and the brakes were heavily ribbed for improved heat dissipation. The new car was not ready for the opening round of the '53 Drivers' Championship in Argentina on January 18 but Fangio was back, joining Gonzalez and Oscar Galvez in '52 machines. Fangio was holding second to World Champion Ascari when his engine blew while Gonzalez and Galvez salvaged third and fifth, respectively.

The A6SSG made its debut at Naples on May 10 where examples were run for Fangio and Gonzalez. Ascari led until his accelerator failed, then Farina forged ahead of Fangio to win while Gonzalez ran home third. Naples' Posillipo circuit was hilly and twisting and the de Dion axle equipped Ferrari scored on grip and handling. At Zandvoort the following month the Maranello

car again had an edge. The circuit had been resurfaced but the track broke up and a large quantity of oil dropped by the Maserati runners in practice made the surface even more slippery.

Maserati ran Fangio, Gonzalez and Bonetto in the Dutch Grand Prix on June 7. Gonzalez took over Bonetto's car during the race, his own breaking a half shaft. He finished third, a lap down while Fangio, unable to keep up with Ascari and Nino Farina retired with a broken rear axle. Two weekends on, the A6SSG was swift enough for Fangio to claim pole position at Spa Francorchamps, a power circuit. Fangio and Gonzalez pulled away from Ascari in the Belgian Grand Prix but both suffered engine failure and Ascari notched up another Drivers' Championship success. Maserati had entered a third car for the Belgian Johnny Claes and Fangio took it over, only to lose fourth on the last lap when he hit oil and crashed out.

Rheims, playing host to the French Grand Prix on July 5 was another power circuit. This time Bonetto's engine failed. Gonzalez tried starting on half full tanks and managed to pull out an impressive lead, but it was insufficient to keep him out of the pack on his restart. Nevertheless, he was able to pip Ascari to third place, in the wake of the leaders. Ahead, Fangio had fought a titanic struggle with young Mike Hawthorn, the Junior in the Ferrari team. Hawthorn could slipstream the Maserati then pull ahead on initial acceleration from the tight Thillois hairpin since Fangio had lost first gear. That was the deciding factor, Fangio losing by a whisker.

On July 18 the British Grand Prix was held at the Silverstone airfield circuit and Maserati ran four cars, adding Fangio's protege Onofre Marimon who had previously been driving a customer A6G painted in Argentinian colours. Ferrari was quickest between the oil drums on the sweeping circuit, Ascari taking pole by a second over Gonzalez who again started on half tanks. He was black flagged for dropping oil but was able to rejoin to claim fourth place while Fangio finished a minute behind winner Ascari, unable to challenge. Bonetto took sixth, Marimon retired.

An even greater Ferrari advantage was evident at the Nurburgring, arguably the supreme test of roadholding, in the German Grand Prix on

August 2. Gonzalez had crashed in a sports car race and was out for the rest of the season: Fangio was supported by Bonetto and Marimon. Ascari lost a wheel but faded star Farina beat Fangio by more than a minute while Bonetto was a distant fourth behind Hawthorn and Marimon had retired.

At Bremgarten for the Swiss Grand Prix on August 23 Fangio claimed another pole position but in the race he quickly faded due to engine trouble and thus took over Bonetto's car, which suffered engine failure. Marimon also suffered engine failure but Bonetto nursed the pole position car home fourth and Hermann Lang brought a fourth works entry home in fifth position.

On September 13 the Italian Grand Prix was held at Monza: here Maserati and Ferrari were closely matched, Ascari, Farina, Fangio and Marimon all featuring in the leading bunch. Marimon suffered a holed radiator but Fangio took the fight right to the finish. Superior acceleration by the four cylinder Ferrari looked to be Ascari's winning edge but Farina wanted to win too and pushed Ascari into a mistake at the last corner, this giving Fangio the verdict. Neither Marimon nor Bonetto finished but the fourth car now driven by youngsters Luigi Musso and Sergio Mantovani came home seventh. At Modena a week later Ferrari declined to enter and Fangio notched up the second major 1953 race win for Maserati.

That gave the marque hope for the 1954 2.5 litre Grand Prix car project on which it had now embarked...

The photographs on the next eight pages show scenes from the 250F's colourful career over the years 1954 - '57. Depicted - in order - are Fangio at Pescara in 1957 (opposite), Behra at Monte Carlo in 1956, Musso at Spa Francorchamps in 1955, Perdisa at Monte Carlo in 1956 and Macklin at Monte Carlo in 1955. Macklin is driving the car privately owned by Stirling Moss , hence its strange green livery.

Working as a team

Maserati's decision to return to Grand Prix racing with the 2.5 litre formula had been made in 1952 and was the bait that had brought the renowned Gioacchino Colombo to Viale Ciro Menotti. As we have noted, Colombo had not only designed the first Ferrari Grand Prix cars, he had earlier fathered the tremendously successful Alfa Romeo 158. Nevertheless, having joined Maserati to design a new Grand Prix car he found himself in the role of administrator. The post of Managing Director suited him far less than that of Technical Director and he left at the end of 1953, before the new Grand Prix car ran, though the engine was tested in a Formula Two chassis.

Colombo had brought young Valerio Colotti from Ferrari and he was responsible for designing the transmission, the chassis frame and suspension of the new car, drawing on his experience of the better handling Ferrari Formula Two chassis. Design and construction of the brand new chassis fell behind engine development.

Of course, Maserati built not only the engine and the chassis structure, but also the aluminium bodywork, the transmission, even the brakes and consequently it had comprehensive technical facilities and a design and development staff with a broad engineering knowledge. It also had a commitment to customer cars for sports car racing as well as Formula One and Formula Two. Medardo Fantuzzi was the competition car body chief, responsible for shaping the racers, albeit on the basis of careful styling rather than any serious aerodynamic testing.

In 1954 J.A. Cooper, correspondent for The Autocar visited the Maserati concern and described it thus: "it is housed in a well built modern factory; it contains machine shops, assembly shops, test house and the usual offices, while heat treatment is carried out there but not foundry work or the actual tubular chassis construction. The bulk of the output of the factory consists of high grade milling machines which have a considerable reputation".

On the racing car side, Cooper found production dominated by the marque's popular 2.0 litre sports-racing car. Engineers Massimino and Bellentani played key roles in the design and development of the new engine and following the departure of Colombo, in August '53 Giulio Alfieri had joined them, and the hundred or so other engineers, technicians and mechanics working in the busy Modena factory. An engine expert, Alfieri came from Innocenti where he had designed two and four stroke engines (and a 125m.p.h. scooter!). However, by the time he arrived the drawings for the new 2.5 litre unit were almost finished.

Cooper noted: "when I queried who was the engine designer, all I could get were shrugs and smiles and the information that it was a Maserati design - "we work as a team!"

Maserati was in easy reach of the Modena autodrome and carried out a great deal of racing car testing at the facility. Chief Test Driver was Guerrino Bertocchi who had joined founder Alfieri Maserati in 1921 and had shared the class winning 1100cc. Maserati in four pre-war Mille Miglias. From the beginning he had been a mainstay of the Maserati racing effort, and he was Chief Mechanic for the factory team.

Clearly, making a complete Grand Prix machine was a formidable undertaking yet Maserati planned its new 2.5 litre runner first and foremost as a production racing car. Ferrari had started out building Formula Two cars for sale to privateers but had found unjustified complaints from poorer drivers disheartening. Inevitably, perhaps, all too often better driven works team cars were unfairly alleged to be faster machines. Maserati would not have this problem since it no longer planned to run factory entries. Instead, it promised works support for its customers with factory engineers in attendance at races.

The sales campaign included a test session for invited drivers of the '53 Formula Two car after the '53 Italian Grand Prix: John Fitch, Louis Rosier, Harry Schell, Roy Salvadori and Mau-

rice Trintignant were among those who took the wheel. Maserati was the only marque offering a serious 2.5 litre contender for the privateer and the list of orders quickly grew. Among them was a car for Fangio, who had tested a new Mercedes in the autumn at Monza but had confirmed that he would be driving a Maserati in '54. The first 2.5 litre engine was not track tested until November, by which time a lot of customers were in the queue and it was obvious that the majority of orders could not be fulfilled in time for the first race to the new formula, to be held in Argentina and in January.

Since the engine was ready well ahead of the chassis Maserati offered A6G Formula Two customers an exchange engine and transmission, producing six so called "interim" cars. Meanwhile it concentrated upon the preparation of the first 250/F1 cars for its two most important customers, Fangio and his rapid protege Marimon, who were backed by the Automobile Club of Argentina. Continuing its relationship with Fangio was a major coup for Maserati. But could it defeat the might of Daimler Benz?

Cramming in Alcohol

84 x 75.0mm./ 2492.5cc
Unblown
Aluminium block and head
Dry iron liners
7 main bearings, plain
Steel crankshaft, 6 pins
Steel con rods
D.o.h.c, gear driven
2 valves/cylinder, 1 plug
46mm. inlet valve, 40mm. exhaust
80 degree included valve angle
Marelli ignition
Weber carburettors
Compression ratio 12.0:1
Maximum r.p.m. 7,500
197kg. including clutch & bellhousing

For its new customer Grand Prix car Maserati logically retained a straight six configuration. With such a cylinder layout the castings for the head and block do not present serious manufacturing problems and it is possible to obtain good rigidity if the proportions are correct. Further, the components are grouped in a manner making for uncomplicated layouts of valve gear, manifolding and ancillaries.

Six rather than eight cylinders were considered adequate given the engine speed Maserati sought for competitive horsepower. The larger cylinder bore was not a problem in terms of piston crown heat flow given the cool running effect of methanol while the possibilities of unrestricted fuel put the emphasis upon the work of the chemist as much as that of the mechanical engineer. Similarly, in years gone by the pursuit of ever higher boost had overshadowed mechanical sophistication, the V16 BRM the exception that proved the rule.

More cylinders promise higher speed but add complication, particularly in terms of the sheer number of parts. Higher speed can also cost reliability while given eight cylinders or more there is also the disadvantage of inherently higher engine weight. Running a 120 degree 'mirror image' six pin crankshaft a straight six is smooth running, with superior balance to an in line four though the length of the 'shaft is such that torsional vibration can present a problem. Of greater concern is the shape of the engine: its length and its height makes it difficult for the chassis designer to package while it is inherently less rigid than a multi-cylinder vee.

Maserati, of course, was on familiar territory with a straight six configuration and went a step beyond the A6SSG with a stroke:bore ratio decreased from 0.945 to 0.893. That implied retention of the original A6G 75mm. stroke together with a bore enlargement from 76.2 to 84mm. Thus, the level of stress measured in terms of piston speed remained comparable while there was the provision for greater valve area. The clever Bowler hat chamber was retained while the valve sizes were duly increased. Again, valve operation was through finger followers with closure of the large valves via triple coil springs. These were subject to rapid deterioration.

Interestingly, while two valves were employed for each cylinder, Massimino had designed an experimental four valve, twin plug in line four Formula Two engine that was never properly developed. Four valves per cylinder added complexity but, significantly, the smaller, lighter valves put less stress on the valve train.

In general the new 2.5 litre engine followed the pattern of the A6SSG. Thus, it was all alloy with a detachable head and a crankcase split at the level of the crank axis while a nitrided steel crankshaft machined from a solid billet ran in seven plain bearings. Roller bearings had been ousted since the war by the reliability of the pressure-fed lead-bronze shell-type thinwall bearings developed by Vandervell, the Formula One entrant. The crankshaft journals were 50.8mm. in diameter carrying 22.2mm. wide intermediate bearings, 28.8mm. wide end bearings.

Again cast iron dry liners, flanged at the top, were pressed into the block which was of closed deck construction. No gaskets were used: jointing compound alone was employed for all metal to metal joints while head to block water sealing was via a circular section rubber strip running in a groove machined into the deck. The crankshaft was again driven by I-section nickel-chrome steel con rods running on plain bearings and it was counterweighted by two balance weights per throw. No vibration damper was fitted. At the small end a 25mm. gudgeon pin ran in a phosphor bronze bush and was retained by wire clips in the four-ring piston.

The piston had a domed crown to achieve a compression ratio of 12.5:1 with deep valve clearance notches. The inlet valve was offset 39 degrees from the vertical, the exhaust 41 degrees. The inlet inclination was three degrees more than seen in the 2.0 litre engine for a larger diameter valve, hence the included angle was 80

rather than 77 degrees. The twin 14mm. plugs were vertically mounted as before.

Bronze based 45 degree valve seats were employed while the finger followers operating the valves were case hardened steel. These followers were pivoted to brackets mounted outside of the respective tappet block to allow withdrawal for clearance setting. The straight tooth spur gear drive from the front of the crankshaft was retained and each camshaft ran in four plain bearings mounted in a detachable tappet block.

Contained in a timing chest at the front of the engine, the gear train again drove the pumps and this time it drove both magnetos. The twin Marelli magnetos were mounted each side of the engine at the front and were driven via an auxiliary shaft. Driven together in this manner, there was no danger of the ignition running out of phase. Three gear type oil pumps were mounted on the timing chest, one pressure and two scavenge, one scavenge for the front of the sump, the other for the rear. A single water pump was mounted low down on the left side of the engine and was driven by a belt from the main gear train. Water was fed separately to head and block, to the former via a six branch manifold.

Three 42mm. twin choke horizontal Weber DCO3s were employed, each cylinder having its own tuned-length trumpet attached to the carburettor body. The exhaust manifolding fed cylinders one, two and three into one manifold, four, five and six into another, twin separate tail pipes being utilised. Compared to a single tail pipe, this reduced the interference between cylinder resonances. The science of inlet and exhaust tuning was still inexact, with less attention paid to harnessing exhaust ram effect by car than motorcycle engineers due to the greater complexity of the problem given four or more cylinders.

Running on a conservative mixture of methanol and petrol and a compression ratio no higher than 12.5:1, the new engine started out producing around 220b.h.p. at a modest 7,400r.p.m. - 90b.h.p. per litre compared to 95 b.h.p. per litre for the faster turning Formula Two engine, albeit with a comparable 11.892b.h.p. per litre per 1000r.p.m. The standard fuel mix was 50% methanol, 35% petrol, 10% acetone, 4% benzol and 1% caster oil. The regular pump petrol was around

The Maserati straight six 2.5 litre Formula One engine for 1954 was derived from the marque's proven 2.0 litre Formula Two six of 1953 and thrived on a blend of methanol and petrol. It produced approximately 220b.h.p. at a conservative 7,400r.p.m. and was intended for privateer use, as the Formula Two unit had been.

80 octane. Acetone made the mix burn faster, reducing the tendency to detonation, while benzol ensured the methanol and petrol mixed properly. Caster oil was necessary since alcohol tends to wash the oil film from a cylinder wall.

This factory specified fuel burned well and thanks to the methanol the engine ran cool and if observant of the 7,400r.p.m. limit a customer could expect reasonable engine durability. Power could easily be increased via a more radical fuel while higher power through higher speed was another obvious development path, again at the expense of more marginal operation thus inappropriate for privateer use. To keep it healthy, the engine needed to be carefully warmed up and a radiator blind was employed to assist the procedure on the track. Initially, in the pits, an experienced mechanic blipping the Webers could feel the right starting temperature via a hand on the cam cover.

Complex with Flex

Maserati chrome molybdenum tubular frame
Unstressed engine
Wishbone independent front suspension, de
Dion rear
Houdaille rotary vane dampers
Borrani 16" aluminium alloy rims
Maserati 13.4" drums, outboard
Maserati twin leading shoes front, single rear
Aluminium alloy bodywork
1 water, 1 oil radiator
Maserati single plate clutch
Maserati four speed gearbox, ZF l.s.d.
200 litre fuel tank, 20 litre oil tank
2280mm. wheelbase; 1300mm. front track,
1250mm. rear.
630kg.

250F on the jig at Modena in 1954, revealing de Dion rear axle.

With its new 250/F1 - this label soon abbreviated to 250F - Maserati took a further step along the path from the simple, flimsy Vintage-style ladder-type girder frame towards the properly-stressed rigid spaceframe ideal of the German chassis theorists. However, it was a small, careful, unadventurous step for the mature company. The new frame it produced was multi-tubular but it was still based on the ladder principle. Its 1mm. wall side rails were of 40mm. rather than 80mm. diameter and this time were in pairs, one above the other with vertical spacing struts between, forming vertical beam structures that increased rigidity in bending. However, it was not significantly stiffer in torsion - if at all - measuring only 300 lb.ft. per degree. For better or for worse, it would therefore inevitably continue to contribute to the hard sprung car's suspension movement.

Parallel and unequal wishbones continued to be employed at the front while Colotti introduced a Ferrari-style de Dion rear axle. The flimsy frame's lower side rails swept upwards front and rear. A pair of tubular cross members (one directly above the other) linked upper and lower side rails at the front; similarly there were two cross members at the rear of the engine compartment and four behind the cockpit, the latter carrying the transaxle assembly. There was also a dash hoop, X-bracing over the scuttle and additional floor and side bracing, this likewise providing against 'lozenging' of the structure. A lighter, non-structural tubular structure extended from the main frame to carry the body panels.

Since the front suspension was carried over from the '52/'53 Formula Two car it was independent with wishbones, coil springs, Houdaille dampers and an anti-roll bar. The unequal length wishbones (162mm. upper, 275mm. lower) were machined from solid steel forgings and were phosphor-bronze bushed. The king pin posts similarly were steel forgings, these joining the outer ends of the legs of the wishbones, the king pin being retained in the post and the stub axle fork bushed to rotate in it.

The lower end of eachcoil spring was mounted on a forged steel cross member bolted to the lower wishbone. The upper end of the vertical coil was located by a fabricated plate welded to the upper frame side member and incorporating a conical rubber bump stop. The anti roll bar passed above this plate and was connected by drop links to the lower wishbone. The Houdaille double-acting rotary vane type shock absorbers were mounted on the chassis between the parallel side members, linked forward to the lower wishbones via drop arms.

The rear suspension was a major innovation for Maserati, following the Ferrari practice of having the de Dion tube mounted in front of the transaxle, rather than behind as per the established, Daimler Benz pioneered layout. The Ferrari layout moved a significant amount of weight ahead of the rear axle, and allowed the fuel tank to be mounted further forward to the same end of improving weight distribution and in particular reducing the moment of polar inertia. The move to a de Dion axle also forced Maserati to adopt a sprung final drive and it located the gearbox in unit with this to the benefit of overall weight distribution.

The de Dion tube carrying the rear hubs was located fore and aft by parallel radius rods running forwards from the hubs to pivots on one of the vertical tubes on the chassis frame. The de Dion tube was located laterally by a ball guide running in bronze-linered steel channel at the front of final drive/gearbox assembly. The ball rocked when one wheel hit a bump and rose/fell under squat/droop. The de Dion did not allow independent action to the rear wheels but kept the wheels upright while cornering, avoiding positive camber which spoils tyre grip. It greatly reduced unsprung weight compared to a rigid beam axle.

The rear springing medium was a transverse leaf spring connected to the two hub carriers. It was situated above the transaxle and de Dion tube at the rear of the chassis frame. It was located laterally by a central leaf clamping plate provided with an external channel section sliding in a pivot pin mounted to the chassis frame rear cross tube. It ran between pairs of rollers set at chassis width, the roller clamps imparting some roll stiffness. In view of that, no anti roll bar was employed. Houdaille double acting rotary vane-type shock absorbers were mounted on plates welded to the lower chassis side members outside the wheelbase with operating arms facing forward and connecting to the suspension via drop links.

The stiffly sprung front and rear wheels were Borrani aluminium alloy rim, wire spoke productions with Rudge Whitworth centre-lock splined hubs. Of 16" diameter they carried Pirelli Stelvio Corse tyres, of 5.5" front section width, 7.0" rear. Pressurised to around 2.25 bar, these high aspect ratio cotton carcase, natural rubber tread tyres were typical of the day and afforded grip that could typically be measured as a coefficient of friction of the order of 0.75 while being prone to overheating if not treated carefully. In spite of its de Dion rear end, thanks to a flexible frame and stiff suspension the 250F was a naturally oversteering car.

At this stage all major Grand Prix cars employed drum brakes though Jaguar had won the '53 Le Mans 24 hour race using disc brakes. Effective discs were a very recent innovation. Maserati's drum brakes were of 13.4" diameter and 2.0" width being in house productions carried forward from the Formula Two programme. Mounted outboard front and rear, the drums were aluminium alloy with unusual transverse rather than circumferential cooling ribs.

The transverse ribs were contained within a dished aluminium plate riveted to the outside of the drum, the ribs arranged as an impeller, drawing air out from the drum. There were also characteristic stiffening and heat dissipating ribs on the back plates both front and rear while the shoes - twin leading shoes at the front - carried shrunk-in and riveted steel flanged liners. The liners were 11in. long providing a total of 92 sq.in. area for the car. Of course, hydraulic operation was retained and a feature of this was the use of twin master cylinders, one for the front brakes, one for the rears, linked by an adjustable balance bar.

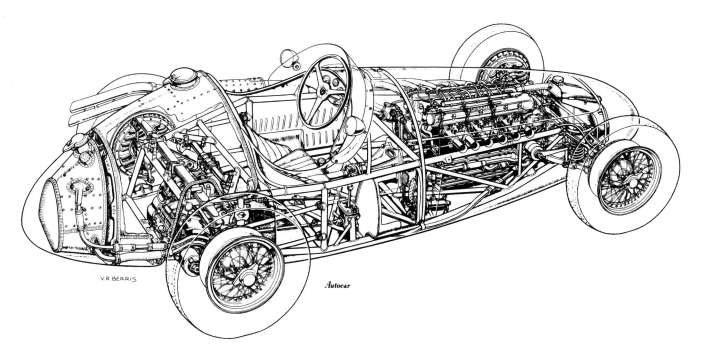

V.R.BERRIS

Autocar

The remote gearbox transmission was new for Maserati but in general followed the principle established by the 1937 Mercedes with a transverse gearbox in unit with the final drive. They were housed in a single Elektron casting that set the de Dion pivot channel on its nose. The engine fed through a new single aluminium dry plate clutch which was attached to the flywheel and was enclosed within a light aluminium alloy bellhousing. The housing had an extended tail bearing to reduce the length of the propeller shaft. A machined face was provided on top of it to carry a bracket on which the steering box was mounted.

The drive was taken to the transaxle via an open prop shaft, this feeding into the new transverse gearbox through a pair of bevel gears, the input positioned on the centreline of the car as was the output. The gearbox was mounted low, beneath the rear wheel axis, and to the right of the final drive and the entire transaxle was attached to the chassis frame via Silentbloc bushes at three points, its installation enhancing torsional rigidity.

The pair of bevel input gears turned the drive through 90 degrees and the transverse layout of the main and layshaft allowed a spur gear differ-

ential drive, a pair of gears raising the drive from the inner end of the layshaft to differential height. Ratio changes were effected by changing pairs of input bevels or output spurs: with five sets of the former and four of the latter there were 20 possible sets of gear ratios, the variation in top speed between adjacent ratios being only about 3m.p.h. In addition it was possible to juggle with wheel and tyre sizes to achieve many more ratio combinations.

The four gearbox ratios were first, 2.14:1; second, 1.45:1; third, 1.20:1 and top 1:1. The gearbox offered four speeds plus reverse and was of the constant mesh type with engagement via dog clutches on the layshaft. All gears were nickel-chrome case hardened steel. The four forward gears were located between two bearings in the main case with the reverse gears overhung outside the end bearings and contained in the end cover which housed the oil feed pump and selector mechanism. The free running gears on the layshaft were on bronze bushes lubricated from the oil pump which was driven off the main shaft so as to maintain lubrication while in neutral. Lubrication of the input bevels and final drive gears was by jets from an external oil pipe. A simple universally jointed gear linkage communicated with the gear lever.

A Z.F. limited slip differential was fitted inside the final spur gear, this differential as first used in racing by Auto Union in the mid Thirties. The ZF unit allowed one rear wheel to spin no more than 15% faster than the other before a system of wedge-shaped cams running between rotating sleeves jammed, locking the differential action. This stopped torque going up in tyre smoke whenever weight transfer loaded the outer wheel at the expense of the inner wheel.

Drive from the differential was via universally-jointed half shafts. Hooke-type joints were fitted to short stub shafts bolted to each side of the differential while pot type joints were splined to the hubs at the outboard end of each driveshaft. Each end of the de Dion tube had a machined housing welded to it, these housings containing two ball races for the wheel hub and pot joint assembly. Machined integrally with the housing was a flange for back plate mounting, also having ears to pick up the suspension links.

Steering was again of the worm and sector type, the worm and sector box was mounted atop the clutch bellhousing, the sector driving a cross-shaft which turned a drop arm on the right. This in turn operated a drag link running alongside the engine, under the carburettors, which worked a bell crank mounted on a front cross member. The bell crank operated a three piece track rod forward of the front wheel stub axles, the drag links attached to the axles facing the front. The track rod ends were phosphor bronze with hardened steel ball joints while the drag links and various slave links were fitted with ball races to reduce friction.

A thick water radiator was mounted very low down ahead of the front suspension and steering system. The main coolant exit channel emerged in the centre of the engine between the cam covers and a fan-shaped header tank linked this to the top of the radiator. A small oil radiator was placed ahead of the water radiator. The oil tank for the dry sump system was mounted to the right of the engine, under the carburettors, attached to the chassis rails.

The fuel tank formed the tail of the car, extending forward over the transverse leaf spring and rear axle assembly, right to the seat back. It was a welded light alloy production of approximately 200 litres capacity. The filler cap projected behind driver's head. A mechanical fuel pump - belt driven off prop shaft - fed the carburettors. There was a facility to fit a five gallon supplementary tank to the right of the cockpit.

Aluminium bodywork shaped the 250F leaving an elliptical orifice to feed the radiator, which was protected by a familiar chrome plated Maserati grille. A small Trident badge was attached to the nose. The bonnet was located via quickly-detachable catches and bonnet and body flanks were liberally louvered to allow hot air to escape. Beneath the bonnet, the flanks of the engine bay offered removable panels to improve service access and a cutaway from the top of the left panel allowed the twin exhaust manifold to escape the engine bay.

The 250F was well clothed, the suspension likewise emerging through close fitting apertures. Aside from the louvers, the model was smooth and it was functional and elegant. It was also of considerable girth, the rear wheels coming close to rubbing the body sides. The frontal area was in the region of 12 square feet. The car had a width of 980mm., a height of 950mm. and an overall length 4050mm. A generous cockpit opening had an aerodynamic wrap around perspex screen rather than the traditional glass aero screen. A perforated heat shield covered the twin exhaust pipes where they passed to the left of the cockpit.

The seating position was upright with plenty of elbow room while feet were spread either side of the bellhousing. The accelerator was inside of the brake pedal to the right of the housing, the clutch to the left. A simple padded seat was positioned above the prop shaft, its leading edge attached to the rear of the bellhousing.

Behind a short scuttle (that straddled the bellhousing) an uncomplicated instrument panel presented a big tachometer and gauges for oil pressure and water temperature. There was also a three position switch for the two magnetos, a chain control for the radiator blind and the chassis identification plate. The gear lever was to the right of the wide cockpit with an H-gate and a lock on reverse. The large aluminium frame steering wheel was wood rimmed with the Trident badge proudly mounted in the centre of it.

*50F straight six seen
Spa Francorchamps
'54 where the works
rs could run to
100r.p.m, the
ivateers to a
aximum of
400r.p.m. However,
nning a works engine
8,200r.p.m. saw oil
zing out everywhere!*

Lost Key

Fangio won the 1954 World Championship with six wins, two of them at the wheel of a 250F. Almost certainly he would have won further victories for Maserati had he not switched to the Daimler Benz camp. Before the delayed arrival of the new Mercedes the two key players, Ferrari and Maserati were well matched and Fangio's superiority over his peers was the Trident's winning edge. The late arriving advanced W196 was clearly superior to the Italian cars only in terms of sophistication: for sheer speed Daimler Benz exploited Fangio's skill, just as Maserati had done. Had Fangio remained at the controls of the 250F, doubtless it would have taken him all the way to the title.

Fangio's Argentinian Grand Prix victory as a quasi-privateer was the impetus for the change of policy that saw Maserati running a works team thereafter. Following the early defection of Fangio Maserati was able to borrow Ascari from Lancia but the reigning World Champion looked uncomfortable in a car that did not give him an unfair advantage over the opposition. More than once he disregarded the red line as he sought to establish status. After just two races he parted company with Maserati, leaving three broken engines in his wake.

Then came the Marimon tragedy at the 'Ring.

DIARY

Buenos Aires (ARG) January 17
Argentinian Grand Prix
Fangio ....1 (Q: 3)
Marimon ....NR (Q: 5)

Although the 250F had not started testing at Modena until December '53 Maserati had managed to ship two examples out to South America in time for this season-opening mid January Grand Prix. Fangio received chassis 2505, Marimon 2502 while four A6GCM-based interim machines were also supplied for the benefit of potential 250F customers. The principal opposition came from the Ferrari team, running what was essentially an enlarged-engine version of its '53 Formula Two car known as the Type 625. Ferrari had lost World Champion Ascari to the as yet unready Lancia Formula One project and had signed Gonzalez alongside Farina and Hawthorn. Aside from the Maserati privateers, the only other competitors comprised a trio of slow Gordinis.

Ferrari's proven package was the most effective at the Buenos Aires Autodrome but intermittent rain played into Fangio's hands. Hawthorn spun and was disqualified for a push start and Marimon spun off leaving Fangio to duel with Farina and Gonzalez. Fangio stopped for hand cut wets as water collected on the track and Ferrari spotted that too many mechanics assisted his tyre change. Sure of Fangio's disqualification, Ferrari slowed its cars as the 250F relentlessly drew away, sliding precariously on the slippery circuit. Fangio was not only the moral victor: Maserati was subsequently fined for the indiscretion but it was pointed out that disqualification was not the automatic penalty for the offence.

Buenos Aires (ARG) January 31

Buenos Aires Grand Prix
Fangio ....NR
Marimon ....DNS in 250F

Marimon crashed 2502 practising for this Formula Libre race. He took over Musso's interim car while Fangio struggled with rear axle problems. In the race Fangio limped in for fresh plugs, only to suffer rear axle failure after nine laps. Ferrari duly took the win courtesy of Maurice Trintignant's private car.

Syracuse (I) April 11
Syracuse Grand Prix
Marimon ....NR
Mantovani............3

Although Maserati had originally stated an intent only to support customer cars, those of Fangio and Marimon in Argentina had effectively been factory entries and an official works team was subsequently run. The factory drivers for this opening non-championship race of the European season were Marimon and Sergio Mantovani. Marimon took an early lead, then half spun causing a pile up behind which eliminated the Ferraris of Hawthorn and Gonzalez. Marimon continued chased by Farina whose Ferrari won after the 250F struck de Dion trouble late in the race, probably a consequence of tapping a wall during the early incident.

Pau (F) April 19
Pau Grand Prix
Marimon ....NR

Marimon was out again at Pau on Easter Monday, only to be hit by Farina at the start and later, probably as a consequence, to suffer de Dion tube failure once again. This non-championship race on a tight street circuit provided a surprise win for Jean Behra's underpowered but nimble Gordini.

Bari (I) May 23
Bari Grand Prix

Marimon..............4
Mantovani ....NR

For the Bari non-championship Grand Prix the factory team was back to two cars. Nevertheless, Ferrari dominated this event. Marimon lay third behind Gonzalez and Trintignant when he had to take on water, dropping him a lap down but he had the consolation of fastest lap.

Castel Fusano (I) June 6
Rome Grand Prix
Marimon 1
Mantovani...........3
Musso ....NR

The non-championship Rome Grand Prix brought a third works 250F for Luigi Musso and no factory opposition from Ferrari. Marimon won (to see his oil tank split as he took the flag) while Mantovani finished third behind Harry Schell's private interim car. Stirling Moss' private 250F had looked set for second but it suffered clutch trouble and the young English hope pushed it over the line for sixth place.

Spa Francorchamps (B) June 20
Belgian Grand Prix
Fangio.................1 (Q: 1)
Marimon...........NR (Q: 4)
Mantovani 7 (Q:11)

The World Championship resumed at Francorchamps after a five month break and Fangio was back in business for Maserati, supported by Marimon and Mantovani. As in Argentina Ferrari provided the principal opposition, the Gordini team uncompetitive here, Lancia and Daimler-Benz unready. Ferrari had a new Type 553 'Squalo' (shark) with a revised, stronger four cylinder engine and a new short wheelbase chassis with saddle tanks which was disliked by the drivers. Farina and Gonzalez drove Squalos at Francorchamps,

Diary continues on page 38

Stirling Moss' private car gave the 250F its first victory in Europe, Moss winning a Formula Libre race at Aintree in May. The Englishman's chassis was 2508, first raced at Bordeaux and from June onwards used for Grand Prix races.

Overleaf are pictured the front and rear suspension of Villoresi's Rheims car, the upper photograph showing the front, the middle the rear. The lower photograph illustrates the first appearance of the rear located oil tank, at the Nurburgring in '54.

Fangio's protege had been rapidly finding his feet and was shaping up as a major Grand Prix driver. Moss was likewise a rising star and the day before the tragedy had been warmly welcomed by Marimon as a new member of the works squad. Moss put his car on the front row of the grid for the German Grand Prix and with the sad loss of Marimon he quickly established himself as the natural leader of the turbulent team. At Monza he held an impressive twenty second lead with just a dozen laps to run when his car failed him.

Moss had started out with a customer deal: one car, one engine. That confined him to a 7,400r.p.m. rev limit at best, 7,200r.p.m. to be prudent, whereas from Francorchamps the works machines were running to 8,100r.p.m. Moss had works engine support from Silverstone and was unlucky there to suffer an unheard of failure of one of the final drive spur gears. Luck was not on Moss' side in 1954. Thereafter, as a full works driver he suffered oil starved engine after oil starved engine. At Bremgarten a retaining nut for a new filler cap worked loose, fell into the oil system and wrecked the oil pump. At Monza an unsupported length of aluminium oil pipe

clamped rigidly against the oil tank cracked the tank around its flange. At Barcelona the oil scavenge pump failed.

Lubrication system problems bugged the 250F in 1954. Motor Sport's reporter Denis Jenkinson later wrote: "Oil pipe unions, pipe runs, pipe joints and so on were all lacking detail design and preparation and the engineers seemed to be completely oblivious to the effects of high frequency engine vibrations on rigidly mounted oil pipes... The Maserati pits could be easily identified by the pools of oil lying on the ground, and it became a reflex action for Maserati mechanics to start mopping up oil as soon as one of their cars stopped at the pits during practice, for if it was not all over the engine, or on the floor of the cockpit, then it was all over the tail".

Oil frothing was the major headache when the 250F made its entrance in Argentina. The car had only tested in a cold Italian winter and the searing heat quickly led to removal of the radiator grille and the appearance of cooling holes in the nose. Since that did not cure the oil frothing the team went to the extent of running the cars on caster oil, buying up most of the stock held by chemists in Buenos Aires! Nevertheless, Fangio's

Diary
Continued

Hawthorn and Trintignant the older Type 625.

Fangio knocked Gonzalez off provisional pole at the end of the first day's practice and thereafter was in charge of the Belgian Grand Prix. However, he made a poor start and Farina led the first three laps. Marimon pitted after one lap and completed only two more, having over-revved on the first lap. After ten laps Farina repassed Fangio but after a short fight the stressed Ferrari engine cried enough and the 250F was left unchallenged.

Mantovani finished at the tail of the field after three plug changes. Two laps ahead, winner Fangio had fastest lap to his credit and had to drive the last couple of laps with a collapsed front suspension. Running private 250Fs, Moss finished a solid third in spite of losing oil pressure, Prince Birabongse Bhanubandh of Thailand who raced under the nom de plume 'B. Bira', finished sixth.

Rheims (F) July 4
French Grand Prix
Ascari .... NR (Q: 3)
Villoresi .... NR (Q:14)
Mantovani .... 5 (Q: 5) *Villoresi*
Mieres .... NR (Q:11)

When the World Championship battle resumed at Rheims two weeks later Fangio was driving one of the new Mercedes cars, costing Maserati its winning edge. Maserati managed to borrow Alberto Ascari and Leo Villoresi from Lancia, the third Italian Grand Prix marque still not ready. Roberto Mieres and Mantovani drove other works Maseratis and, short of equipment, the factory had to borrow Moss' machine for Villoresi, Moss racing a Jaguar sportscar in the companion race.

Mercedes wheeled out three enclosed wheel streamliners for Fangio, Karl Kling and Hans Herrmann while Ferrari had Squalos for Gonzalez and Hawthorn, a 625 for Trintignant. Fangio took pole position while Kling was a second slower and just one tenth of a second ahead of Ascari who had run his engine over the red line. Ascari made a poor start and blew his engine on the first lap: the Silver Arrows ran away, Fangio and Kling chased by Gonzalez whose engine blew after a dozen laps. Mieres and Villoresi joined the long list of retirements with transmission and engine failure respectively and Villoresi took over Mantovani's car to finish three laps down. The best Maserati could manage was fourth for B.Bira's customer car.

Silverstone (GB) July 17
British Grand Prix
Marimon 3
Ascari .... NR
Villoresi .... NR (*Ascari*)

Maserati had to start from the back of the grid having arrived too late for official practice due to a shipping error. Moss, however, had put his private car an impressive third on the grid. This season the young English privateer had really started impressing the Grand Prix circus. At Silverstone he was running as a quasi-works entry and he was able to run higher revs given the promise of replacement engines. The works cars were driven Ascari, Villoresi and Marimon while Mercedes again had a trio of streamliners and Ferrari three 625s with the Squalo engine. A host of British and French make-weights padded out the field.

Gonzalez used the revised Ferrari to good effect, winning while the unconventional Mercedes floundered somewhat between the oil drums. Meanwhile, Ascari suffered a steering problem then a dropped valve, took over Villoresi's car and saw a con rod through the block of that. However, Marimon finished a strong third from his lowly starting position,

ahead of Fangio but a lap down on Gonzalez. Hawthorn was second after the demise of Moss who suffered a broken de Dion tube. Moss shared fastest lap with Marimon, Ascari, Gonzalez, Hawthorn (who brought his 625 home second), Behra (Gordini) and Fangio.

Nurburgring (D) August 1
German Grand Prix
Marimon .... (*Q: Accident*)
Villoresi .... (*Q: Withdrew*)
Moss .... (*Q: Withdrew/ Reverted to private status*)
Mantovani .... (*Q: Withdrew/ Reverted to private status*)
Mieres .... (*Q: Withdrew/ Reverted to private status*)

Moss' Silverstone drive had further impressed Maserati and he became a full works driver for the German Grand Prix, his green car duly painted red. Ascari had left but other works cars were unloaded for Villoresi and Marimon while Mantovani and Mieres were running private cars under the factory umbrella. Prior to the race Daimler-Benz had hurriedly prepared three open wheel versions of its W196 and these were entered for Fangio, Kling and veteran Lang. Herrmann drove a streamliner while Ferrari fielded four 625s, Gonzalez and Hawthorn having the revised versions.

Tragically, Marimon suffered a fatal accident during qualifying and as a sign of respect Maserati withdrew from the race. Moss, Mieres and Mantovani ran as private entries but Moss and Mieres retired early, the former with engine failure after holding a strong third place behind Gonzalez and Fangio. Fangio soon demoted Gonzalez and dominated the rest of the race while Mantovani finished fifth, behind a mixture of silver and red cars.

Oulton Park (GB) August 8
Gold Cup
Moss 1

Diary continues on page 40

oil pressure was running dangerously low when down came the cool rain to dampen his anxiety...

Oil frothing later recurred in Europe and the problem was eventually identified as the location of the oil tank, too close to the engine. The answer was to relocate the tank at the extremity of the tail, where it was serviced via untidy external piping. This modification was introduced for the German Grand Prix and it was the failure of the new system that cost Moss his Monza win, the Englishman employing it there for the first time.

Another early weakness was lack of strength in the de Dion tube. Tube failure cost Moss his chances in the May Silverstone International Trophy and he had a replacement made for his private car in England from better quality steel. Later the factory increased the wall thickness from 1.5mm. to 3.5mm. producing a heavier but stiffer and stronger tube. Similarly, the transaxle input bevels had to be beefed up, the originals too heavily loaded for their size and prone to stripped teeth.

Detail modifications were an improved fuel pump, a riveted rather than welded fuel tank (seen along with the relocated oil tank, in Germany) and a new wire mesh grille superimposed with a large Trident badge, though this was often discarded. At Barcelona the prototype car appeared with the oil lines to the rear tank properly plumbed through the fuel tank and fitted with cooling fins, and with side slots rather than louvers to exhaust hot air from the engine bay. This was the car driven by Godia-Sales.

At Monza a new exhaust system was tried in practice with inconclusive results, this having further blending into a single large bore tail pipe. The real development for performance came from a new cylinder head, introduced for the works cars at Francorchamps. It featured larger inlet valves and new camshafts and together with strengthened con rods was the key that took peak power to 8,100r.p.m. By 8,200r.p.m., however, the engine was showing signs of stress with oil leaking profusely!

Clearly the driver had to use the performance with discretion, which Ascari was unwilling to do. Perhaps Ferrari engines took more abuse. Fangio on the other hand drove the second half

Diary Continued

Maserati supplied Villoresi's Nurburgring car for Moss to race on home soil, against Behra's Gordini and various British privateers. Having missed official practice he had to start from the back of the grid but with Behra on five cylinders there was no real opposition for him.

Pescara (I) August 15
Circuit of Pescara
Moss .... NR
Musso 1

Again with factory opposition only from Gordini, Moss was by far the fastest but this time he retired early on with a broken gearbox oil pipe and Musso won, beating B. Bira after the private 250F required attention to its brakes with only one lap to run. Bira had the consolation of fastest lap.

Berne (CH) August 22
Swiss Grand Prix
Mantovani .... 5 (Q: 9)
Moss .... NR (Q: 3)
Mieres 4 (Q:12)
Schell .... NR (Q:13)

The following weekend four works cars were out in the Swiss Grand Prix at Bremgarten, the drivers Moss, Mantovani, Mieres and new recruit Harry Schell. Daimler-Benz (running three open wheelers), Ferrari (with three revised 625s) and Maserati - all the serious runners - were closely matched in practice, Gonzalez fastest, two tenths quicker than Fangio, nine tenths faster than Moss. Moss was quickest of all in the wet but the race was dry. Nevertheless, he lay second to Fangio in the early stages only to drop back then retire with oil pump failure, leaving Gonzalez to chase Fangio home. Schell

also retired but running steadily Mieres and Mantovani finished fourth and fifth respectively.

Monza (I) September 5
Italian Grand Prix
Mantovani .... 9 (Q: 9)
Villoresi .... NR (Q: 6)
Moss .... 10 (Q: 3)
Musso .... NR (Q:14)
Mieres .... NR (Q:10)

The Italian Grand Prix found Moss, Villoresi, Mantovani, Mieres and Musso heading the Maserati challenge, all but Villoresi driving their own cars under the factory wing while French privateer Louis Rosier had a works car on loan. Ferrari had a further revised 625 driven by Ascari (still the Lancia was not ready) plus earlier revised 625s for Hawthorn and Trintignant and a standard 625 for Fagioli. Mercedes had streamliners for Fangio and Kling while Herrmann drove an open wheeler. In practice Fangio was only two tenths faster than Ascari, three tenths faster than Moss after a rousing duel between the Italian and the Englishman.

The 80 lap race was closely matched, too, with Fangio, Kling, Moss, Ascari, Hawthorn, Gonzalez and Herrmann all well in contention in the opening laps. Gonzalez, Herrmann and Kling were soon in trouble while Villoresi came up well to join Moss who was running a comfortable third to Ascari and Fangio. Surprisingly, Villoresi went ahead of Moss but quickly his clutch failed. Meanwhile, Mantovani came up ahead of Hawthorn.

Soon after half distance Moss assumed the lead, then Ascari retired. That left Moss comfortably ahead of Fangio with Mantovani and Hawthorn scrapping for third. Alas, as Moss strode on towards his first Grand Prix victory an oil system failure caused his engine to run its bearings. Pushing his car over the line to a standing ovation, he completed only 71 laps. Fangio was handed a lucky win. Mantovani suffered a broken de Dion tube: he stopped after 74 laps.

Goodwood (GB) September 26
Goodwood Trophy
Moss 1

The short Goodwood Trophy race offered no continental factory opposition for Moss who won in convincing style, setting a new Formula One lap record for the circuit.

Aintree (GB) October 4
Grand International
Moss 1
Mantovani 4

A stronger cast at Aintree but Moss was still in a class of his own while, following the demise of Behra's Gordini, Mantovani was beaten by Hawthorn in Vandervell's home brewed Vanwall Special and Schell's private 250F. A Formula Libre race at the end of the day saw the works Maseratis first and second after the demise of Vandervell's 4.5 litre Thinwall special Ferrari driven by Peter Collins.

Pedralbes (E) October 24
Spanish Grand Prix
Mantovani .... NR (Q:10)
Moss .... NR (Q: 6)
Musso .... 2 (Q: 7)
Mieres 4 (Q:11)
Schell .... NR (Q: 4)

Maserati regrouped and the factory team was out again in force for the final World Championship Grand Prix of 1954, the Spanish race in Barcelona. The drivers were Moss, Mantovani, Mieres, Musso and Schell while a revised chassis was lent to Spanish driver Francesco Godia-Sales. Daimler-Benz entered two open wheelers and a streamliner while Ferrari had a modified 625 for Trintignant and a Squalo for Hawthorn. At last the Lancia was ready to race and D.50s were handled by Ascari and Villoresi, the former taking pole position. Moss shunted in practice and Ascari was joined on the front row by

Diary continues on page 42

of the Francorchamps race nursing his engine. His mechanical sympathy and the lack of pressure from Ferrari allowed that win.

Even running to 8,100r.p.m. it appears that the power output of the Maserati straight six did not exceed 240b.h.p. The target figure of 100b.h.p. per litre was just that tiny bit out of reach: while power went up with the extra revs, it did not increase in terms of b.h.p. per litre per 1000r.p.m. and the revs could not go high enough to reach 250b.h.p. Indeed, it appears that peak power was produced at 8,000r.p.m. the breathing inadequate to continue the climb of the power curve with additional revolutions.

Running a maximum 7,400r.p.m. with the original head, privateers were lucky to see 220b.h.p. Moss's car was measured in England as producing a realistic 214b.h.p. at 7,200r.p.m. on 50% methanol and there it ran out of breath, the horsepower figure no greater at 7,400r.p.m.

Nevertheless, the 250F was always very competitive on sinuous circuits, suggesting a broad power band and good road holding. The major chassis improvement of 1954 came right at the start of the season: to improve the handling scuttle cross-bracing tubes were cut away. This imparted a degree of flexibility that made the car more controllable. Clearly, the 250F was a supple machine and this made it very effective in the wet. The Owen Organisation measured the torsional rigidity of the chassis it purchased and registered a figure of only 250lb./ft. per degree.

In spite of its lack of torsional rigidity, in the dry the model handled well enough, though it was a 'slider' rather than a 'sticker', having a strong tendency towards oversteer. The 250F was born to drift. Since contemporary tyres offered low levels of grip this was not wasteful of time, nor did it cause excessive tyre wear. Altering tyre compounds and, more commonly, tyre pressures was the way to tune the handling. Pirelli's tyres were particularly well suited to the car and Moss found it necessary to ditch his stock of Dunlops to make his private car go quickly.

Prior to the European season Maserati introduced an alternative longer wheelbase, up from 2200mm. to 2280mm. With its coil spring independent front suspension, its leaf spring de Dion rear end and its 'flexible' frame working in

harmony the 250F was well balanced. Moss noted: "It steered beautifully, and inclined towards stable oversteer which one could exploit by balancing it against power and steering in long sustained drifts through corners. It rode well on the normal type of relatively smooth-surfaced course, although its small coil springs and leaf spring rear-end would use up available suspension movement over the bumps at the 'Ring".

Certainly, the 250F was a forgiving car and this made it well suited to privateer use. Total production ran to a dozen cars in 1954, half going into private hands. In all the model won 11 races in 1954, the vast majority minor Formula One events at which, in the absence of the latest Ferraris and the Mercedes, it was typically the class of the field.

The prototype machine - 2501 - ran at Modena Autodrome in December '53 until hit by a spinning sports car, which caused heavy damage. Thus two more chassis were hastily completed for shipment on December 26, the factory even working the morning of Christmas Day. Fangio's car in Argentina was 2505, Marimon's 2502 and both examples were subsequently taken into the official works team. Chassis plate 2503 was reserved to replace Schell's interim car of the same number but he didn't manage to get the finance together and consequently the number was never allocated. However, B. Bira replaced his interim A6GCM-2504 with a 250F of the same number. 2506 was another '54 factory team car and like 2505 it won first time out, being Marimon's Rome winner.

Chassis 2507, 2508 and 2509 all went to English customers, Sid Greene's Gilby Engineering concern taking 2507, Moss 2508, the Owen Organisation 2509. Chassis plate 2510 was another reserved to replace an interim car that the owner - in this case Baron de Graffenried - didn't get around to trading in.

Since the chassis number was also carried by the engine and the interim cars ran borrowed 250F engines it was logical they should take over the chassis number. In total there were five interim cars, the two others A6GCM-2501 and - 2502. A6GCM-2501 was Mieres' car and he, of course, was drafted into the works team. The damaged 250F prototype re-emerged at the 1954

Diary Continued

Fangio, Hawthorn and Schell who planned to start on a half a tank and act as hare.

Schell ran hard for 29 of 80 laps, battling with Hawthorn and Trintignant after the demise of Ascari (joining Villoresi in retirement), then his gearbox seized. Moss had already fallen out due to oil system failure while leading Fangio. Ferrari was left comfortably placed first and second.

Trintignant's Ferrari hit trouble while running second but there was no denying Hawthorn the win. Overshadowed by the faster Italian cars, Fangio was heading for second when an oil leak intervened, leaving a press-on Musso the runner up. Mieres was fourth, close behind Fangio's sick car and Godia-Sales was sixth, followed home by three 250F customer cars. Mantovani should have been up with Musso but shunted after suffering locked brakes.

The four cylinder Ferrari engine pictured at the 'Ring in '54. It is a development of the Formula Two engine with which Ascari won the 1952 and '53 World Championship titles. Having only four cylinders facilitated Ferrari's efforts at inlet and exhaust pipe tuning.

Gonzalez' Squalo Ferrari leads Moss' 250F in the Italian Grand Prix at Monza. Moss soon passed the Ferrari - which retired early - and went on to take a commanding lead, only to suffer oil system failure.

Paris Salon and was not raced until Barcelona. A6GCM-2502 belonged to Jorge Daponte and he ran under the wing of the factory in Argentina when Marimon was racing 'his' rush-built 250F of the same number. However, Daponte was another interim owner not to upgrade, hence the inclusion of 250F 2502 in the official factory team after its Argentinian sortie.

250F chassis 2511 was supplied to Mantovani in August, by which time he was part of the works team while 2512 was introduced the same month at the 'Ring for Marimon and was the car in which he was killed. It was subsequently rebuilt. Chassis 2513 was sold to the Vandervell organisation less engine and was not delivered until December. Chassis 2514 - the last of the '54 batch - had earlier been phased into the works team, at Monza.

The only real difference between the works cars and those of the customers was the engine. For most privateers longevity was the primary consideration. Typically a customer ran his car frequently throughout the season and sometimes even lived off the starting money. He therefore hoped to run a number of races between major engine rebuilds, keeping to 7,200r.p.m. On the other hand, in the face of the serious opposition from Ferrari and Daimler Benz the 8,100r.p.m. works engines were nothing if not highly stressed.

The four cylinder Ferrari that started the season was little different from the marque's '53 Formula Two car aside from having a stroke:bore ratio of 0.957 rather than 0.866, its dimensions of 94mm. x 90mm chosen for logistical reasons. It had two twin-choke Webers, twin plug ignition and a four into one exhaust system. Running on a conservative 80:20 petrol:alcohol mixture the 625 engine gave a quoted 230b.h.p. at 7,500r.p.m. though since that represents 12.26 b.h.p. per litre per 1000r.p.m. one suspects the figure somewhat optimistic. Power was allegedly increased to 245b.h.p. during the course of the season, though such a figure at 8,000r.p.m. would clearly call for something stronger than 80% petrol in the fuel tank.

Meanwhile, Ferrari introduced the Squalo four cylinder, again designed by Lampredi. This car had a bore and stroke of 100mm. x 79.5mm. - a stroke:bore ratio of 0.795 - for higher speed and larger valves. The revised engine had twin plugs and although to the established pattern featured certain detail changes. It was not a success, lacking bottom end rigidity.

There were also major chassis modifications in the production of a Squalo, including a more elaborate multi tubular frame. The wheelbase was shorter, the fuel was carried in saddle tanks and the de Dion axle was set ahead of the transaxle, 250F style, all of which which made for a very low moment of polar inertia. However, the Squalo at first proved dismally unreliable and the drivers disliked the handling of the compact machine with so much of its weight within the wheelbase. The twitchy car demanded a new driving technique.

Ferrari's initial response was to combine the head of the Squalo with the bottom end of the 625 and to put the hybrid engine into the 625 chassis. It later tried the bottom end from the Type 735 Monza sports car. This hybrid engine was used in the Squalo chassis at the Swiss Grand Prix then a Squalo engine was tried in the 625 chassis at Monza. Finally, for Barcelona there was a modified Squalo with coil spring front suspension.

Evidently, in the face of the problems facing the Squalo design the Ferrari engineers lost direction during the course of the season. Nevertheless, the team was generally a match for Maserati and Mercedes and it took Grand Prix wins at Silverstone - Gonzalez in a 625 with the first hybrid engine - and at Barcelona - Hawthorn in the modified Squalo.

Daimler Benz likewise had its problems, aggravated since its W196 was heavy and somewhat complex. Unlike Maserati and Ferrari the bigger German company came into 2.5 litre Formula One with a fresh sheet of paper and a lot of fresh ideas. It had a bigger budget than available to either Italian team yet its highly scientific and highly professional approach did not relegate the red cars to the status of also ran.

The W196 employed a straight eight engine which was canted over almost onto its side to overcome the inherent disadvantages of the configuration, those of a high bonnet line and a high centre of gravity. In traditional Mercedes style the engine had an integral head construction, welded steel water jackets and a long built-up crankshaft running in low friction roller bearings and with ball race big ends (driven by one piece con rods). In view of the length of the unusual 'shaft the engine was constructed as two banks of four with a central power take off and timing drive.

There were two overhead camshafts and two valves per cylinder at an included angle of 90 degrees servicing a conventional hemispherical twin plug chamber. The cylinder dimensions were 76.0mm. x 68.8mm. - a stroke:bore ratio of 0.905 and a potential for 9,000r.p.m. before piston speed became dangerous. The valves were opened and closed positively via an ingenious desmodromic system of cams and rockers, hence speeds in excess of 9,000r.p.m. were possible without the valves contacting the pistons, together with more generous valve openings.

The W196 employed Bosch direct fuel injection leaving its porting unrestricted, yet for all its sophistication its b.m.e.p. was only average and its peak power speed was no higher than 8,500r.p.m. (albeit with over-revving not a danger thanks to the desmodromic system). At that level power was quoted as 256b.h.p. which represents 12.05b.h.p. per litre per 1000r.p.m. Judging by the car's track performance the power band was not unusually wide and the level of power attained was no significant advance over the Maserati six, or the Ferrari four, for all the engine's impressive complexity. Indeed, for the engine speed possible the engine performance was disappointing.

The Mercedes chassis was similarly sophisticated - arguably over-engineered - with a very well triangulated, stiff multi tubular frame, inboard drum brakes and torsion bar suspension employing a swing axle layout at the rear. The brakes were of a new design with both shoes moving outwards about their whole length instead of pivoting at one end. Mounting them inboard not only reduced unsprung weight but also enabled the provision of wider drums with more generous finning. Nevertheless, braking performance was not above reproach this season.

The equally innovative swing axle design ensured independent wheel control together with a low roll centre and was based on production car technology. With its stiff frame and sophisti-

Left: scenes from Rheims 1954, the engine bay of the new Mercedes W196 (note the wide inboard drums) and Kling (20) and Fangio en route to victory, passing Salvadori's abandoned Gilby Engineering 250F. Salvadori is seen right chasing Wharton's BRM V16 at Goodwood on Easter Monday on the debut of his car, chassis 2507. The two cars later collided. Above, Mantovani is depicted at Spa Francorchamps, where sadly he only lasted a few laps of the race.

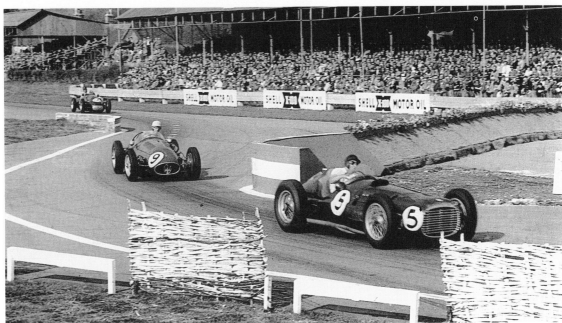

cated suspension, the W196 chassis was theoretically a major advance over its Italian rivals. But again paper potential did not translate into a tangible advantage on the track. The W196's inherent understeer was fashionable but scrubbed speed. Further, the car did not handle well at the Nurburgring, that most testing of circuits. Only flat out at Rheims did the Mercedes look a step beyond the Italian cars.

Wind tunnel tests had evolved a low fully enveloping body with an impressive drag coefficient. Although it presented a greater frontal area than a similar height open wheeler it was claimed to be worth an overall 20% reduction in drag. Nevertheless, the car did not show a marked advantage at Monza and earlier, at Silverstone the streamlining had proved a liability. In 'The Grand Prix Car' Setright has suggested that this might have been due to a conflict between the inherent understeer and an high speed aerodynamic oversteer promoted by the body shape. The Silverstone experience brought forward development of the alternative open wheel style with more predictable handling.

Daimler Benz deserved to win first time out at Rheims but Moss was the moral victor at Monza. The open wheel car won at the Nurburgring and Bremgarten through Fangio's skill rather than any technical superiority. Even with exposed wheels, the over-engineered W196 was clumsy and the 250F was a far more driveable car than either it or the difficult Squalo. The 250F was an immensely practical racing car rather than a drawing board winner and after Francorchamps lacked only the sparkle of Fangio.

Technically speaking, the car of the year was the Lancia. The all new, late arriving V8 car was not as radical as the W196 but it was innovative with fully stressed engine, outrigged fuel tanks and other more subtle features. More importantly, it was light, held the road well and had a very wide power band. Little that was innovative in 1954 was destined to change the face of Grand Prix technology and in the final analysis light weight, good grip, good handling and useable power were as achievable by time honoured tradition as by any new approach tried this season. But in the new lay long term development potential.

On the previous page is the first corner of the '54 German Grand Prix, Gonzalez leading having made a superb start in his Ferrari. Next is Fangio's W196, then Moss' private 250F ahead of the W196s of Lang and Herrmann, the latter in a streamlined version. Fangio won the race.

Lancia did not race its fascinating D.50 until the last Grand Prix of the season, the Spanish event at Pedralbes. This is Ascari in the pole winning car which he retired early. Note the distinctive outrigged pannier tanks keeping the heavy fuel load out of the tail.

French Connection

In 1954 Alfred Neubauer, the Mercedes Team Manager, had advised young Stirling Moss to go racing as a privateer and 'earn his spurs'. By the end of the season Moss had established himself as a major force in Formula One and Maserati looked to him to lead its 1955 challenge. However, Neubauer had also been impressed and asked Fangio how he would feel about having the Englishman as his teammate. Fangio: "I told them he was the best driver they could take. For me it would have been better to have a mediocre driver beside me... Instead I chose the best, because when I race a particular car I am racing for the car and the team".

All of which left Maserati again in the lurch. Maserati felt that the loss of Fangio to Mercedes had cost it the '54 title and here was Stuttgart luring away its '55 hope. Of course, Moss could not afford to miss the opportunity of joining the most heavily funded, most highly regarded works team of all. He retained his private 250F which he would drive in certain lesser events but he was lost to the Modena factory squad.

Maserati cast around and signed as Team Leader Neubauer's second choice after Moss: Jean Behra. Although he didn't have the sheer natural ability of Fangio or Moss, Behra had tremendous courage and an equal share of determination. He was also fiercely patriotic. He had never given up the struggle in the underpowered blue cars but there was clearly no way that the small Gordini concern could give him a competitive Grand Prix mount. Sensibly moving down to Modena, Behra was joined by rising Italian star Luigi Musso, gifted Italian amateur Sergio Mantovani and Roberto Mieres from Argentina, all of whom could be counted upon for solid support.

These days a growing sports car racing programme was testing the resources of the Maser-ati competition department, which was undergoing something of an upheaval. Towards the end of '54 Bellentani had moved down to Maranello to replace Lampredi and Massimino had also quit, to act as chassis consultant to Ferrari. Alfieri assumed the post of Technical Director, with responsibility for road and racing cars. Under his direction Maserati looked to increased engine potential, the chassis remaining essentially unchanged with the bodywork without louvers fitted to 2501 at Barcelona standardised.

Alfieri later told historian Doug Nye: "Fangio was always very soft, very gentle on the car. In a race he would consume 10 to 15 litres less fuel than the others, wear his brakes less and all the other parts of his car too. After he had gone, the others in comparison were all very hard, rugged on the cars, and we had to make them stronger - but we wanted them lighter and more powerful as well".

Chassis were mainly carried forward from '54 and no new customer cars were constructed. Private entrants continued to be serviced by the factory's racing department which consequently became somewhat hectic during the season. Many owners based their mechanics in Modena so that they could work on their charge at the factory. When the factory ran short of chassis it was known to be prepared do a deal with a customer, allowing it to temporarily change the chassis plate and fit a works engine. Indeed, it has been suggested that the factory once or twice borrowed a customer's car in this manner without his knowledge!

Jean Behra's determination was used to Maserati's good effect in 1955. Here the Frenchman is pictured at Spa Francorchamps where he ran fifth early on, only to spin into a ditch just before La Source.

Standing Still

In 1955 Daimler Benz moved forwards, Maserati stood still. The W196 might have been on the same footing as the 250F in 1954 but it logically had a greater development potential and that potential was realised in 1955. Meanwhile, Maserati lacked the driving talent to fully exploit the performance of the well honed 250F. Not that Team Leader Behra and in particular plucky young Luigi Musso gave up all hope and there were memorable performances, such as at Zandvoort.

Alas, after the Argentinian season opener the heroics were invariably played out in the wake of the two top drivers of the year driving the top car fielded by the top team. Behra won at Pau and Bordeaux but the best results against Daimler Benz were third places at Monte Carlo and Zandvoort. The 250F sometimes looked potentially as fast as the W196 and its main assets were its simplicity - though reliability was still patchy, possibly due to the team trying to overstretch itself - and its sheer 'driveability'.

Daimler Benz had a combination of ample engineering expertise and ample resources with which to humble both Maserati and Ferrari. The Italian teams employed perhaps two dozen works

Buenos Aires (ARG) January 16
Argentinian Grand Prix
Behra ....NR (Q: 4)
Mantovani...........7 (Q:19)(Behra/
Musso)
Mieres 5 (Q:16)
Musso ....NR (Q:18) (Schell)
Schell.................6 (Q: 7) (Behra)
Menditeguy.......NR (Q:13)
Bucci ....NR (Q:20)
(Menditeguy/Schell)

Again the World Championship season commenced at Buenos Aires in January and this year's race attracted strong works teams from Maserati, Ferrari, Lancia and Daimler-Benz, with a clutch of Gordinis to add variety. Maserati entered the new line up of Behra, Mantovani, Mieres and Musso plus, on a temporary basis, Schell, Carlo Menditeguy and Clemar Bucci. Ferrari replied with further modified Squalo engined 625As for Gonzalez, Farina, Maglioli and Trintignant while Lancia had D.50s for Ascari, Villoresi and Castellotti; Daimler-Benz, W196s for Fangio, Moss and Kling.

Each marque was represented on the front row of the grid, Gonzalez on pole seventh tenths faster than Behra who was also pipped by Fangio and Ascari. The race was held in searing heat and was primarily a test of stamina for the drivers: only Fangio and Mieres were able to run without relief. The Maserati challenge was spoiled by fuel pump failure: no less than seven pumps were changed during the race.

Behra suffered a split oil tank following an incident on the third lap which claimed Menditeguy's car and he took over from Mantovani. Meanwhile, in the early stages Schell and Mieres ran very strongly, Schell taking the lead as the

taxed Fangio stopped for water to be poured over him. Having found little joy with Mantovani's car, Behra then took over the Schell car, losing the lead to Fangio in the process as Mieres was set back by fuel pump replacement. Menditeguy meanwhile had taken over from Bucci and Schell moved to this car.

Half distance saw Fangio leading Behra in Schell's car. Schell then retired the Bucci car, then took over Musso's car which likewise failed. It was then Behra's turn to hit trouble - but not terminally - while Musso had a go in Mantovani's delayed car. Both these cars came home, behind solo runner Mieres who took a well deserved fifth place.

Buenos Aires (ARG) January 30
Buenos Aires Grand Prix
Behra.................5
Menditeguy 6
Mantovani ....7 (Schell/Musso)
Schell.............. NR
Musso ....8 (Schell)
Mieres........... NR

For this two heat Formula Libre race Daimler Benz prepared 3.0 litre engined cars while Behra had an enlarged, 2.7 litre Maserati. The first heat saw Farina's regular 2.5 litre Ferrari beat the Mercedes trio with Gonzalez' Ferrari fifth, the 250Fs overshadowed. Schell's engine had failed and he had taken over from Mantovani. In the second heat Musso, Menditeguy and Behra challenged the Mercedes as the Ferrari favourites failed. However, Trintignant brought his Ferrari through to third, close behind Fangio and Moss with Schell and Behra next up.

Turin (I) March 27
Valentino Grand Prix
Behra ....NR
Musso............NR
Mieres 2
Perdisa ....NR

The European season commenced at Turin on March 27 with a confrontation be-

tween Maserati, Ferrari and Lancia. Maserati fielded Behra, Mantovani, Musso and Mieres but in practice Mantovani crashed heavily. A leg amputation proved necessary, ending his career. His place in the team on race day was taken by youngster Cesare Perdisa. Musso led until he came under pressure from Ascari and spun into retirement. Mieres took second to the Lancia while both Behra and Perdisa suffered broken de Dion tubes.

Pau (F) April 11
Pau Grand Prix
Behra 1
Musso .... NR
Mieres 3

The non championship Pau Grand Prix attracted works cars for Behra, Musso and Mieres to face factory entries from Lancia and Gordini. Second in qualifying, Behra had a modified engine but could not keep up with pole man Ascari, though he led him over the opening laps. However, the leading Lancia found trouble late in the race giving the Frenchman another Pau victory. Mieres was third behind Castellotti's Lancia while Musso retired.

Bordeaux (F) April 24
Bordeaux Grand Prix
Behra 1
Musso.............2
Mieres 3

For Bordeaux both Behra and Mieres had the revised engine. Lancia was absent but Ferrari fielded its heavily revised yet disappointing new Squalo, the Type 555 'Supersqualo'. Maserati dominated the three strong front row, Moss putting his private disc-braked 250F alongside Behra and Musso. Moss' disc brakes caused trouble in the race, as did a broken fuel tank retaining strap. That left the works trio unchallenged, Behra leading home

Diary continues on page 54

52

First lap of the Dutch Grand Prix at Zandvoort: Fangio's W196 leads Musso's 250F, Moss' W196, Kling's W196 and Behra's 250F. Moss soon forged past Musso but the Italian finished hard trying third for Maserati.

team members. Daimler Benz had 270 people concentrating upon Formula One. In signing both Fangio and Moss it had cornered the market in driving talent to boot. The sophisticated Silver Arrows - which even had cockpit control of rear shock absorber settings to compensate for a diminishing fuel load - were found generally to be enhanced via a shorter wheelbase which pushed the front brakes outboard.

Indeed, they were prepared in different guises to suit individual circuits - with the choice of short, ultra short, medium or long ('54) wheelbase - and although still somewhat clumsy to drive were extremely effective. The chassis performance was adequate, not outstanding but the fuel injected engine at least lived up to its sophistication.

Power was quoted as 280b.h.p. at 8,700r.p.m. - 12.87b.h.p. per litre per 1000r.p.m, a figure achieved running nitromethane which is a costly but effective way of upping b.m.e.p. More impressive was the relatively high peak power speed while this year high power was combined with a very wide power band ensuring effective engine performance regardless of circuit characteristics. All of which left the essentially 1954 specification, bigger braked, 240b.h.p. 250F over

shadowed, as was the rival Ferrari. Fuel with a higher methanol content could take Maserati over 250b.h.p. at the cost of excessive fuel consumption.

If anything, the Ferrari 'Supersqualo' was even more fully eclipsed than the 250F. The Supersqualo featured a revised chassis with a compromise layout that put more fuel in the tail without removing the saddle tanks. The move was not a success and with the 625 model long in the tooth Ferrari was happy to take over the Lancia D.50 project.

The Lancia had arrived too late in 1954 to make a valid comparison against that season's runners. Nevertheless, Ascari had managed to put the D.50 on pole at its one and only appearance, in Barcelona. Clearly, the car had potential. As we have noted, like the Mercedes W196, the D.50 was a clean sheet of paper design and it represented another fresh approach to Grand Prix car design. However, at the heart of its philosophy was a desire to minimise the moment of polar inertia that echoed the work of Lampredi with the Squalo.

The D.50 was the work of Vittorio Jano, the acclaimed engineer who had done so much for the glory of Alfa Romeo between the wars. It

Diary
Continued

Musso and Mieres. Both of the unimpressive Supersqualos retired.

Naples (I) May 8
Naples Grand Prix
Behra 4
Musso 2
Mieres .... NR

This time the Maserati trio faced the Lancias of Ascari and Villoresi. Ascari was again in charge and on this occasion he was victorious, chased home by Musso. Behra overtook Villoresi only to suffer hub damage through contact with a kerb, which left him fourth at the finish. Meantime Mieres had fallen by the wayside.

Monte Carlo (MC) May 22
Monaco Grand Prix
Behra 3   (Q: 5) (Perdisa)
Musso .... NR   (Q: 8)
Mieres .... NR   (Q: 6)
Perdisa .... NR   (Q: 11) (Behra)

The serious business of World Championship racing recommenced in the streets of Monte Carlo with strong teams from Maserati, Lancia, Ferrari and Daimler-Benz and slower Gordini and Vanwall runners to add interest. In the Maserati camp, Perdisa again joined Behra, Musso and Mieres in 250Fs while Fangio and Moss were joined by Andre Simon after Herrmann crashed in practice. The two star Mercedes drivers had special short wheelbase chassis. Lancia fielded a quartet of D.50s while Ferrari had four cars and only two were the unloved Supersqualos.

Fangio and Lancia drivers Ascari and Castellotti headed qualifying with Behra next up, continuing to show good form. However, since only the first day's times

counted for the grid he lined up behind Moss' Mercedes as well. From the start the two quickest Lancias chased the two quickest Mercedes with Behra in hot pursuit. By one third distance Behra was ahead of the Lancias, the silver cars far distant. Alas, before half distance the 250F's engine went off song.

Musso had retired after only eight laps with transmission failure but as Behra slid down the order Mieres was elevated to fifth, behind Ascari and Trintignant's Ferrari. Then Fangio retired the leading Mercedes and Behra swapped cars with Perdisa, rejoining in seventh place. Mieres moved ahead of Trintignant only to retire - another transmission failure - and with the demise of Moss and Ascari Trintignant was handed a lucky win. Behra spun and retired Perdisa's car from third place but Perdisa limped home third, a lap down, the only Maserati finisher.

Spa Francorchamps (B) June 5
Belgian Grand Prix
Behra .... NR   (Q: 5)
Musso 7   (Q: 7)
Mieres 5   (Q:13) (Behra)
Perdisa 8   (Q:11)

Ascari's Monaco retirement had taken the form of a spectacular trip into the harbour - his car sinking to the sea bed - and four days later he had crashed testing a Ferrari sports car in unexplained circumstances. That accident had cost his life and had prompted the withdrawal of Lancia. Only one D.50 ran at Francorchamps, a privately entered but works fettled machine for Castellotti. Ferrari sent three of the difficult Supersqualos while Mercedes had three open wheelers, Maserati its usual quartet with the lone Vanwall to add a splash of green.

With an almost empty tank Castellotti took pole position while Musso started from the back as his car refused to fire under starters orders. On full tanks Fangio and Moss smartly pushed the quick Lancia down to third while Farina's Ferrari and Kling's Mercedes led Behra. Alas,

before long Behra spun out of the race. He took over Mieres' car, which was running ninth, while Musso was the best placed 250F, taking his turn to challenge Kling.

At half distance Musso lay fourth, behind the runaway Mercedes and Farina's Ferrari, the Lancia having retired. Behra was now seventh, a lap down. Over the second half of the race Behra gained ground and Musso required a plug change and lost ground. Behind the unchanged leading trio Kling retired and Paul Frere kept his Ferrari ahead of Behra for fourth place while a disappointed Musso finished behind Trintignant's Ferrari.

Zandvoort (NL) June 19
Belgian Grand Prix
Behra 6   (Q: 6)
Musso 3   (Q: 4)
Mieres 4   (Q: 7)

The month of June brought the terrible Le Mans tragedy which led to the cancellation of a number of races. Only the Dutch, British and Italian Grands Prix were left on the World Championship calendar.

Zandvoort saw Castellotti join Ferrari and Hawthorn rejoin after an unhappy time with the latest Vanwall challenger. Of the British car, there was no sign. Ferrari's third runner was Trintignant and again Maranello sent Supersqualos. Mercedes replied with its regular trio of Fangio, Moss and Kling while Maserati sent cars for Behra, Mieres and Musso.

Musso was best of the rest in practice, the three Mercedes dominating the front row. Behra made a better start than Musso to snatch second to Fangio but at the end of the first lap Musso was second, though Moss soon demoted him. The race settled down with Fangio and Moss leading Musso and Behra while Kling fended off Mieres who had fastest lap to his credit. Unsuccessfully, since the W196 spun out. Behra stopped to investigate his handling but Musso and Mieres continued to fly the

Diary continues on page 56

54

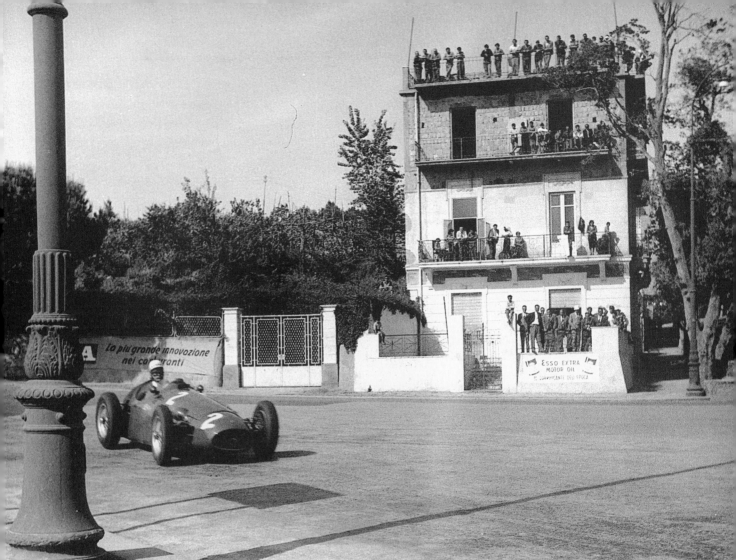

Behra at Naples in the Naples Grand Prix, a non-championship race held in May. He finished fourth, five laps down on winner Ascari's Lancia. However, Musso's 250F ran troublefree, finishing second.

was very compact and employed both its V8 engine and its transverse transaxle as heavily stressed members of the chassis, which was otherwise multi-tubular. The front suspension was conventional, with leaf springing and tubular dampers, as employed at the rear. The front suspension was hung on a front sub frame then the engine formed a portion of the chassis, with just two small diameter floor tubes running back to the scuttle superstructure.

The engine was set at a slight angle to the longitudinal axis of the car to offset the propshaft alongside the driver's seat for a lower seating position. The wheelbase was short and the clutch was integral with the transaxle, which otherwise echoed the 250F layout and offered five forward speeds with Porsche-type synchromesh on the top four.

The transaxle was designed to carry the rear axle which was de Dion with an unusual central location. A guide ball ran in a channel but the ball was linked to a bracket beneath the tube rather than directly to it. This arrangement served to lower the roll centre. The de Dion tube curved behind the transaxle. However, there was little weight of fuel in the tail since the majority was carried in the distinctive pannier tanks, outrigged on aerofoil-section struts and positioned between the wheels.

As with the original Squalo, the fuel location ensured the handling stayed consistent as the fuel load diminished while the unique panniers - only just exceeding the frontal area of the front wheels - promised to beneficially clean the airflow between the front and rear wheels. The compact layout, in particular the short wheelbase and the pannier fuel location ensured the D.50 was very agile with a very low moment of polar inertia and it demanded a new style of driving. There was little warning of breakaway

Diary Continued

Italian flag, Ferrari completely overshadowed.

Aintree (GB) July 16
British Grand Prix
Behra ....NR *(Q: 3)*
Musso ....5 *(Q: 9)*
Mieres ....NR *(Q: 6)*
Simon .... NR *(Q: 8)*

The British Grand Prix saw Simon replace Perdisa in the 250F works line up while Mieres had a new five speed gearbox. Ferrari had the three runners seen at Zandvoort while Mercedes added a fourth car for Taruffi. Vanwall bounced back with two cars and other rabbits of note included Jack Brabham's sports car bodied Climax-Cooper. In practice Behra split the four Mercedes with Mieres next up and that was the order on the first lap, Fangio leading Moss with Musso in sixth.

Once more Fangio and Moss were in full command, Moss winning on this occasion. Behra chased the Silver Arrows but early on his engine failed while Mieres split the two slower W196s until he too lost his engine. Mercedes were then left with the top four positions, Musso finishing fifth after leading Taruffi much of the way. Simon had retired early, unable to select gears. Meanwhile Ferrari had again been overshadowed.

Monza (I) September 11
Italian Grand Prix
Behra................4 *(Q: 6)*
Musso............NR *(Q:10)*
Mieres...............7 *(Q: 7)*
Mengiteguy.........5 *(Q:16)*
Collins...........NR *(Q:11)*

At Zandvoort and Aintree Ferrari had been floundering but prior to the Italian Grand Prix it was handed the redundant Lancia cars. It planned to race the D.50s on the newly combined road and banked circuit but tyre failures in practice saw it revert to four Supersqualos. Mercedes fielded streamliners for Fangio and Moss backed by open wheelers for Kling and Taruffi while Maserati had a new streamlined car for Behra.

Although the streamliner ran hot, Behra was a full second quicker than Mieres in the best of the regular cars but he was still 3.6 seconds slower than poleman Fangio. Fangio and Moss were joined by Kling's open wheeler on the front row with Castellotti next up in a Supersqualo then a gap where Villoresi should have lined up a Lancia, Behra heading the third row.

At the end of the first six mile lap the four Mercedes led Castellotti, Hawthorn and Mieres with Behra only tenth, behind 250F newcomer Collins. Collins found trouble early on and Musso emerged as Maserati's best hope, working his way up to fifth running in close company with Castellotti. By half distance Musso was fourth, Moss having been set back by a broken windscreen while Behra was now sixth, behind Castellotti. Moss recovered from eighth to pass Behra only for his transmission to fail.

Then tyre trouble struck Musso leaving Castellotti to move into third as Kling retired. Only the three leaders finished with healthy cars, Behra finishing fourth in a cloud of smoke as a piston had failed, ahead of Mengiteguy who moved up well in the late stages. Mieres struggled home seventh overcoming engine trouble.

Oulton Park (GB) September 24
Gold Cup
Moss 1
Musso............NR
Gould ....NR

The Italian Grand Prix had been the last race for Daimler Benz' W196 equipped Grand Prix team, leaving Moss free. He rejoined Maserati, replacing Behra who had been injured in a sports car race while two other works cars were sent to England, for Musso and regular 250F privateer Horace Gould. The principal opposition came from Hawthorn and Castellotti in Lancia-Ferraris while the Vanwalls of Titterington and Schell held the second row, the order on the first Hawthorn, Moss, Musso, Castellotti.

The Lancias were quickest off the mark but Moss assumed the lead on the first lap and went on to a comfortable win. Musso came through to second, only for his gearbox to fail late in the race. Gould retired with engine trouble.

Syracuse (I) October 23
Syracuse Grand Prix
Musso 2
Villoresi 3
Shelby .... NR
Piotti ....NR
Schell.............. NR

The final works outing of 1955 was the non-championship Syracuse Grand Prix. Unopposed by Ferrari, Maserati entered Musso, Villoresi, Carroll Shelby and Luigi Piotti in regular cars plus Schell in the Monza streamliner. Nevertheless, dental student Tony Brooks driving his first Formula One race in the underpowered Connaught totally eclipsed this formidable force. Troubled by his brakes, Musso finished fifty seconds behind the young upstart, who had been slowed by his team.

and once the limit of adhesion - which was high- was reached all four wheels tended to lose adhe- sion at once.

Jano's V8 engine had a 90 degree vee angle and a conventional two plane crankshaft. At its heart was an aluminium alloy monobloc carrying wet iron liners and providing the upper housing for each of five (plain) main bearings. The main bearing caps were firmly bolted up into the half- skirt monobloc, with four bolts per cap. Thus the sump was non-structural, the monobloc and the detachable heads playing the role of chassis. The heads provided hemispherical combustion cham- bers serviced by two plugs and two valves, the latter operated directly through mushroom tappets.

The valve angle was 80 degrees included and the twin overhead camshafts were chain driven. Four twin choke Solex carburettors and two magnetos were employed. The cylinder dimen- sions were 73 x 73mm. and power output was reckoned to be a competitive 250b.h.p. at 8,400r.p.m. which was the speed at which it moved into the dangerously high region of pis- ton speed of over 4000 feet per minute. Signifi-

cantly, there was plenty of mid range punch relative to the standards of the day. However, the real potential of exhaust pulse tuning for a 90 degree V8 engine had yet to be realised.

Although the D.50 had not appeared until Barcelona it had first been aired in February '54 and the long delay hinted at the over- ambitious nature of Lancia's Grand Prix ambitions. The early part of the '55 season saw the D.50 pose the most serious threat to the Silver Arrows, though there is no doubt that the car was tricky to drive at the limit. Then it all turned sour in the wake of Ascari's death testing a Ferrari sports car, following his plunge into the harbour at Monte Carlo. That watery trip in a D.50 came as he attempted to gain ground on the leader.

Meanwhile, Lancia was tumbling into a finan- cial nightmare and the family company was duly sold to a financier. There was no question of continuing the marque's participation in Grand Prix racing but such was the car's obvious po- tential that Fiat offered to finance Ferrari to carry on the fight. Jano joined Ferrari and Lampredi left. The D.50s eventually reappeared for the Italian Grand Prix only to suffer tyre failures on the Monza banking, this problem intensified by running 16" rather than 17" rear wheels. In 1955 the cars only raced under the Ferrari badge in the Oulton Park Gold Cup which was won by Stirling Moss in his private 250F.

That triumph hinted at what might have been, had Moss been based at Modena rather than Stuttgart in '55. He wouldn't have had the sheer resources to have enabled him to topple Fangio - let alone the experience - but doubtless he would have given Maserati a greater share of the glory. Interestingly, this season his private car carried a number of significant modifications.

In 1954 the Owen Organisation car had been equipped with corners by Dunlop: Dunlop tyres, Dunlop wheels and Dunlop disc brakes, as used by Jaguar to win Le Mans in 1953. The Moss car likewise wore Dunlop magnesium alloy wheels and discs in '55, saving a total of over 10kg. unsprung weight. The outstanding feature of the disc brake was its freedom from fade under high temperature operation, thanks to the exposed disc offering a higher rate of cooling. Further, it transferred less heat to the tyre, another important consideration. Both Owen and Moss disc conversions proved a success.

The main feature of Moss' car, however, was SU fuel injection, an indirect, low pressure diesel engine system specially adapted for the private car by the SU experimental department. Given the fact that methanol fuel is relatively insensitive to mixture strength, injection was, on the face of it, a straightforward option, one that promised to better match fuelling to engine speed and load.

The SU injection pump was driven at half engine speed from the exhaust camshaft, its rate of delivery responding to both speed and load. Load measurement involved fitting a plenum chamber over the inlet trumpets, at the open front end of which was placed a single throttle butterfly. The forward facing plenum produced a beneficial ram effect and the pressure was measured in the back of it. The pressure connection was arranged to override the straight line delivery characteristics of the pump delivery plungers. Injection was into the port.

The injection system increased peak power from 214b.h.p. at 7,200r.p.m to 232b.h.p. at 7,400r.p.m. on 50% methanol - an impressive

Maserati wheeled out a streamlined version of the 250F for the Italian Grand Prix, run on Monza's combined road and banked course. The car is seen in the pits on the previous page and left on the banking, Behra at the controls.

12.5b.h.p. per litre per 1000r.p.m. By increasing the methanol content to 85% at the expense of significantly higher fuel consumption the power was raised to 253b.h.p. at the same speed - a truly impressive 13.67b.h.p. per litre per 1000r.p.m.

With the SU injection fuelling was superb at maximum speed, as is illustrated by the gain in power between 7,200 and 7,400r.p.m. the engine finding nothing over 7,200r.p.m. on carburettors. The sharp increase in power with a high alcohol content suggested the engine was under-valved, methanol carrying its own oxygen. This is consistent with the fact that the works cars had been fitted with a big valve head early in '54 and that even bigger valves came this season.

However, the improved top end performance with the SU system came at the expense of a markedly narrower power band and very poor response. In essence, the pump simply could not be made to respond quickly or well enough to changes in load and speed and fuelling was not optimum throughout the rev range. Even with

85% methanol power fell off between 4,500 and 6,000r.p.m. compared to the Weber engine, hence the significant loss in terms of the width of the power band. In the light of this the SU system was quickly dropped.

The factory cars did not try either disc brakes or fuel injection, although Alfieri was doing research into these areas with a view to future application. The modified works carburettor engine was introduced early in the season at Pau, having larger valves together with appropriately revised porting and matching Weber 45 DOC3 (45mm.) twin choke carburettors plus inlet stacks which were longer as well as wider. The bigger bore carburettors were mounted flexibly rather than rigidly.

Power was quoted as 260b.h.p. at 8,000r.p.m. - 13.0b.h.p. per litre per 1000r.p.m, this splendid bench reading hinting at the use of a high alcohol content. At the same time useful power was available over a wider band thanks to progress in terms of inlet and exhaust tuning. The single tail pipe was standard from Monza this year as

Having failed to shine at Monza, the 250F streamliner re-appeared at Syracuse at the end of the '55 season. A strong Maserati team for this non-championship race was humbled by newcomer Brooks' low power Alta-Connaught.

exhaust tuning became more refined while a slightly downdraught carburettor arrangement was introduced along with it.

This year there were larger fuel pumps driven via a belt from the prop shaft. Monza also saw the introduction of wider front brake drums for greater lining area. However, the major chassis innovation of '55 was a new five speed gearbox, with which first gear was not in constant mesh, being designed only for starting.

Its deployment facilitated the use of a high final drive for fast circuit work. First seen at Aintree this 'box became standard equipment for the works team at Monza.

Three new chassis were built in 1955, all for the works team: 2515, 2516 and 2518. The number 17 is considered unlucky in Italy. The works team also employed chassis 2501, 2512 and 2514 suitably updated. Mantovani, of course, was lost to the team early in the season and he was replaced by Cesare Perdisa. Andre Simon and Louis Rosier joined the list of customers, buying ex- factory cars 2505 and 2506 respectively. During the course of the season Bira sold his car to Horace Gould.

Chassis 2518 was the special wide streamlined car seen at Monza. Unlike the Mercedes streamliner the Maserati low drag special had been designed without reference to wind tunnel testing, by the usual process of styling for function, through intuition. The base car was higher than the W196 and the new full width body did not attempt to fully enclose the tyres. It presented a sports car type nose that left the tips of wheels exposed and filled in the space between the

wheels, extending the regular body out to the the full width and height of the nose.

At the rear fins were positioned behind the wheels and these were linked to the standard tail profile via downward sloping decks. Scoops in the nose fed the front brakes while cutaways in the side let hot air escape. The exhaust ran under the new side panels, emerging just behind the cockpit. Alas, the hot enclosed pipe run tended to set fire to the paintwork above when stationary in the pits, unless the body was doused by cold water!

Neither at Monza nor at Syracuse was 2518 a success, though it apparently gave Behra a slight advantage over his teammates in the Italian Grand Prix. At Monza 17" rear wheels were run in view of the stresses imposed by the banking and the conflicting demands of the banked and road sections of the course compromised tyre performance. That limited everyone's ultimate speed on the Italian Grand Prix circuit.

Syracuse was, of course, the scene of the ignominious defeat of Maserati by young Tony Brooks in a new Alta-Connaught. Although the British car was notable for its use of disc brakes, it was on acceleration rather than under braking that it scored.

The four cylinder Alta engine had a bore and stroke of 93.5mm. x 90mm. - a stroke:bore ratio of 0.963 - and a conventional hemispherical head with two valves. These were at an included angle of 72 degrees and were operated through rocker arms by chain driven twin overhead cams. The engine was aluminium alloy with cast iron cylinders playing a structural role and only three (plain) main bearings. As with the Alta Formula Two engine from which it was derived, very careful attention had been paid to inlet and exhaust tuning and although SU injection had previously been employed the Syracuse winner had two twin choke carburettors.

The Alta ran to only 6,400r.p.m., producing a quoted 240b.h.p. which represents an unrealistic 15b.h.p. per litre per 1000r.p.m. While true maximum power is therefore unknown, it is clear that the engine boasted a commendably fat power curve. Allied to a light chassis which held the road well and got the power down well, there lay Brooks' advantage. Food for thought over the winter.

The 250F sported a new drum brake at Monza in '55 which was wider for more lining area. Brakes were continually uprated throughout the life of the car.

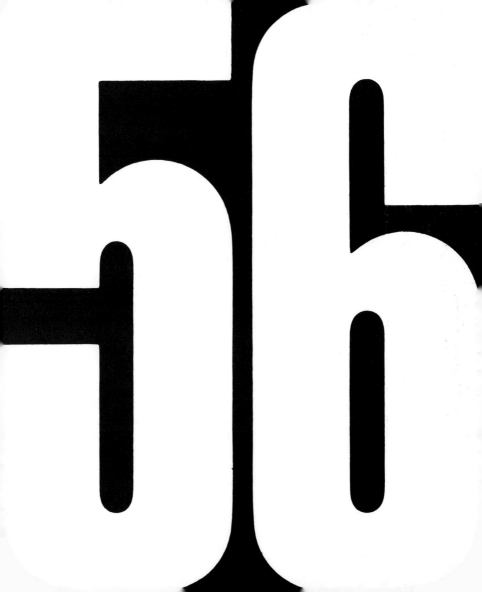

Power Shift

The withdrawal of Daimler Benz allowed Maserati and Ferrari to breathe a sigh of relief for the German company had set a standard of excellence that neither Italian stable had the resources to match. Further, it released the two top drivers, Fangio and Moss. Fangio was seriously considering the possibility of retirement but the fall of the Peron government presented him with many business problems. He reluctantly returned to Europe and accepted a tempting offer from Ferrari. Ferrari, of course, had the Lancia cars that had presented the most serious challenge to the W196 in 1955.

Meanwhile, Moss accepted an offer to lead the Maserati team, though not before trying the three British contenders - the Connaught, the Vanwall and the BRM. So far only Connaught had come out of the midfield shadows, with its Syracuse win. Patriotism wasn't enough: Moss knew that only the Italian teams were capable of providing him equipment that would give him a realistic chance of winning the 1956 World Championship.

Musso moved to Ferrari but in his quest for Fangio's crown Moss was ably supported by Behra and Menditeguy, who was part of the Maserati sports car racing team. For Behra the '55 season had finished in hospital following a huge crash in the Dundrod TT race. The accident left him with a plastic ear.

For the new season Nello Ugolini moved from Ferrari to act as Team Manager. The sports car racing effort was still growing and was increasingly a burden on the competition department. The Formula One cars initially prepared for the new season were from the existing stock, up rated with still wider drums that boasted wider and deeper stiffening cross-ribs. Five speed gearboxes were now used by private entrants and a couple more customer cars were under construction, to be followed by a batch of new chassis for the works team.

The major development effort went into fuel injection, following the lead set by Moss' private car in '55. Fuel injection and disc brakes - also run by Moss' 250F - were the two great innovations of the mid Fifties, though both technologies had been around a long time. Alfieri was planning to toy with discs during the '56 season. He faced the problem that neither suitable fuel injection nor disc brake systems were produced by Italian companies such as Weber and Pirelli, causing logistical difficulties.

Maserati 250F straight six pictured at Spa Francorchamps in '56. From this race the radiator air was ducted out through a slot at the front of the bonnet in the interest of improved aerodynamics.

Wind Cheaters

Moss reckoned that he had learned more in '55 from following in Fangio's wheeltracks than he had learned in the preceding three seasons. Facing Fangio as the leader of the rival camp he was a worthy adversary in the quest for the '56 World title. During the season the technical advantage swung back and forth between Maserati and Ferrari but throughout the 250F lacked top speed and too often it let Moss down when it really counted. Fangio made his World Championship hat trick in spite of a problem of poor car preparation early in the season. Moss won two Grands Prix and finished runner up.

In 1955 the Lancia D.50 had looked to have a distinct advantage over the 250F, together with more long term development potential. That promise was not realised under the sign of the Prancing Horse. Nevertheless, the engine, which Jano continued to develop, appeared to be stronger than that of the Trident stable. At Rheims Ferrari introduced an over square version developed by Bellentani, displacing 76mm. x 68.5mm. - a stroke:bore ratio of 0.901 - and using nitromethane power reached 275b.h.p. at 8,400r.p.m. - 13.10b.h.p. per litre per 1000r.p.m.

The chassis, on the other hand, was modified away from Jano's original philosophy so as to reduce the cornering power of the rear wheels

DIARY

Buenos Aires (ARG) January 22
Argentinian Grand Prix

Moss .... NR   (Q: 7)
Behra 2   (Q: 4)
Menditeguy .... NR   (Q: 6)
Gonzalez .... NR   (Q: 5)

Although the 1956 World Championship season predictably opened in Argentina, before the event Moss won a New Zealand Formula Libre race in his private 250F. At Buenos Aires the Englishman was backed by Behra, Menditeguy and burly Jose Froilan Gonzalez, a figure rarely seen these days. The Modena factory cars were in familiar trim. In opposition Ferrari had a mixed bag of Lancia and Supersqualo based equipment for Fangio, Musso, Castellotti, Gendebien and Collins, Fangio driving a modified D.50 in which he took an easy pole position.

This Grand Prix was fought solely by Ferrari and Maserati. Musso took the lead at the start, chased by Gonzalez and Menditeguy both of whom passed the Ferrari driver on the first couple of laps. Menditeguy took the lead and Gonzalez was passed by Fangio, only for Fangio to pit. However, Gonzalez' car then went off song and Moss came up to second in spite of suffering an injury to his feet. Castellotti led the Ferrari challenge and Fangio took over Musso's car, rejoining fifth behind Behra.

Soon Fangio was fourth, then third as Castellotti retired. Ahead, Moss met engine trouble then Menditeguy was put off by a gear selection difficulty. Moss eventually retired leaving Behra to follow Fangio home. Hawthorn brought the Owen Organisation's 250F home third, while Gonzalez fell out with engine failure.

Mendoza Autodrome (ARG) February 5

Buenos Aires Grand Prix

Moss 2
Behra 3
Menditeguy 4
Gulle 8

Two weeks later battle was rejoined at a new circuit, Mendoza Autodrome high up in the foothills of the Andes near the border with Chile. The Ferrari team had the upper hand, the 250Fs losing more power in the thin air. Fangio, Castellotti and Musso made the running chased by Moss, Behra and Menditeguy. However, Musso crashed out and Castellotti retired as a stone punctured his oil radiator. But there was no denying Fangio the win. Menditeguy looked set for third until he lost a cylinder or two while slow local driver Pablo Gulle brought the ex-Gonzalez car home eighth, five laps down.

Goodwood (GB) April 2
Glover Trophy

Moss 1

Moss came out at Goodwood on Easter Monday with an experimental indirectly injected works car facing British based cars including three Connaughts and two BRMs. Hawthorn led initially in a BRM then the race came down to Moss versus Archie Scott-Brown's Connaught, the Connaught leading. Moss followed until half distance then found a way past as the British car - slightly faster on the straights - ran into braking difficulties. Thereafter the Maserati was untroubled. Both Scott-Brown and Hawthorn retired and Salvadori's private 250F was a distant second.

Syracuse (I) April 15
Syracuse Grand Prix

Behra .... NR

Again, at Syracuse on April 15 an injected factory car was run as an experimental entry, this time for Behra. On this occasion the opposition included the works Ferrari team with four cars, plus Connaught and Gordini with two apiece. Behra

was third quickest in practice, behind Fangio and Castellotti who led at the start. Behra ran fifth behind the works Ferraris and retired early with a broken oil pipe. Castellotti retired and fourth fell to Villoresi in a works assisted 250F, who was followed home by Gerini in a similar car.

Monte Carlo (MON) May 13
Monaco Grand Prix

Moss .... 1 (Q: 2)
Behra .... 3 (Q: 4)
Perdisa .... 7 (Q: 7)

Running with a regular engine, unsupported by the factory, Moss had won the Aintree 200 on April 22, then the weekend before Monaco he won the Silverstone International Trophy for Vanwall. Meanwhile, Maserati had concentrated on its fuel injection development. The works team was out again in force for the Monaco Grand Prix, in which Moss was supported by Behra and Perdisa, all in carburettor cars. Menditeguy was missing following a sports car accident and the only injected engine was in a spare car.

Ferrari replied with modified Lancias for Fangio, Castellotti, Collins and Musso while other works entries came from Vanwall, BRM and Gordini. Vanwall had its totally revised Silverstone winning model and useful drivers in Harry Schell and Maurice Trintignant. BRM withdrew after practice with valve trouble but Schell's fifth fastest showed that the Green was to be taken seriously this year. Meanwhile, Fangio was fastest of all, six tenths ahead of Moss while Behra lined up behind Castellotti.

Moss jumped into an immediate lead and went on to win without a serious challenge. Early on Fangio spun out of second, taking Musso out and leaving Collins to chase Moss. Fangio recovered to third while Castellotti's clutch disintegrated, taking the pressure off fourth man

Diary continues on page 68

relative to the front and thus make the car more driveable. The exercise was inconclusive. Ferrari relocated the bulk of the fuel load in the tail of the car, retaining only small reserve tanks in the front ends of the panniers. The panniers themselves were blended into the body, slightly increasing the frontal area but by no means automatically increasing drag. It is possible that interference between the body and the original outrigged panniers had actually increased form drag.

The four exhaust pipes each side passed through the vacated space in the panniers to emerge just ahead of the rear wheels. The rear leaf spring location was revised, a front anti roll bar was fitted and Houdaille rotary vane replaced tubular shock absorbers. From the start of the European season the reserve tanks were moved from the panniers to the sides of the chassis frame.

Fangio had to work hard for his success in Argentina, then was squarely beaten by Moss at Monaco. The 250F was running as at Monza in '55 with a single bore tail pipe and the five speed

gearbox and Monaco saw the introduction of a revised cylinder head with 10mm. rather than 14mm. plugs which allowed some redesigning of the combustion chamber. This season the Maserati was occasionally burning nitromethane and power was then reputedly in the region of 270b.h.p. at 8,000r.p.m. - 13.50b.h.p. per litre per 1000r.p.m.

While the engine could run to well over 8,000r.p.m. without breaking, these days power reached 240b.h.p. at a conservative 7,300r.p.m. Equally as important, peak torque was registered at only 5,500r.p.m. and the power band was extremely wide by the standards of the day.

Nevertheless, at Spa Francorchamps - with additional streamlining - Moss could get ahead of the modified D.50 only in the wet and at Rheims he could not challenge it at all. On these ultra high speed circuits the Vanwall made a good showing. The British car had a distinctive low drag aerodynamic body and a powerful in line four engine - a match for Italian horses - but the emerging challenger was not yet ready to

Behra's Maserati 250F pictured at the British Grand Prix carrying an auxiliary fuel tank. This took space alongside the engine originally occupied by the oil tank.

Behra. Perdisa was then fifth. At quarter distance Fangio moved up to second but he ran into clutch slip. His own car weakening, Fangio took over Collins' mount but was too far behind to better second. Behra took a steady third a lap down while Perdisa was seventh after suffering a grabbing brake.

Spa Francorchamps (B) June 3
Belgian Grand Prix
Moss .... NR   (Q: 2)
Behra................ 7   (Q: 4)
Perdisa 3   (Q: 9) (Moss)

Prior to the Belgian Grand Prix Moss had taken time out to win a minor race at Crystal Palace in London in his own car, then it was on with the serious business in the Ardennes. Maserati had a rebodied, low drag car for Moss, plus an experimental direct injection engine that proved powerful but too heavy on fuel, calling for an extra pit stop. Moss reverted to carburettors. Again he was backed by Behra and Perdisa who drove regular cars while Ferrari fielded four modified Lancias, and loaned an example to local Gordini driver Andre Pilette. Vanwall continued to keep the Red Army on its toes.

Fangio was comfortably quicker than Moss in practice but Moss led the early stages on a damp track, chased by the three fastest Ferraris, the two Vanwalls then Behra. On lap five, as the track dried Fangio took command. Moss stayed in touch only to suffer a broken hub. That left Ferrari filling the top three positions chased by Behra. Soon Castellotti retired then Moss took over Perdisa's ninth placed car and broke the lap record getting back onto the lead lap. At half distance he lay sixth, soon that was fifth.

Ahead, Frere's Ferrari challenged Behra hard and this became a duel for second as Fangio's rear axle broke. Behra then suffered engine and gearbox maladies leaving Moss a distant third with fastest lap to his credit, the last finisher on the lead lap. Behra was still running at the finish but had a water leak, falling back to seventh - lucky to see the flag. Collins won.

Rheims (F) July 1
French Grand Prix
Moss .... NR   (Q: 8)
Behra 3   (Q: 7)
Perdisa 5   (Q:16) (Moss)
Taruffi .... NR   (Q:12)

Moss drove the low drag car again at Rheims, backed by Behra, Perdisa - running an injection engine - and Taruffi. Ferrari fielded five modified Lancias with bigger bore engines while Vanwall, which had shown promising speed if poor handling at Francorchamps, lined up Schell and returnee Hawthorn. Gordini and a new Bugatti project carried the Blue. Surprisingly, the improving British Racing Green cars lined up behind the three quickest Ferraris: Behra was the top 250F runner in sixth position, just ahead of Moss. Unlike Vanwall, Maserati did not have the speed to challenge this weekend.

The three quick Ferraris made the running while the Vanwalls were soon in trouble, as was Moss. A broken gear lever sidelined his car and he replaced Perdisa in the injection car, restarting ninth. Meanwhile, Behra had fallen back to sixth and Schell had recovered Vanwall's position strongly, moving into the lead. For the British hope that was too good to last and general attrition gave Behra third place at the flag behind Collins and Castellotti while Moss was fifth, two laps down. Taruffi retired with engine trouble.

Silverstone (GB) July 14
British Grand Prix
Moss .... NR   (Q: 1)
Behra 3   (Q:13)

Perdisa 7 (Q:15)
Godia 8 (Q:25)

Two weeks later the British Grand Prix at Silverstone saw BRM add to the British challenge, Hawthorn putting his example on the front row. However, Moss was on pole, this weekend running a regular 250F and backed by Behra and Perdisa in similar cars with Godia making up the numbers. Fangio and Collins sandwiched the BRM, then on the second row came Roy Salvadori in the Gilby Engineering 250F whose impressive time was matched by the Vanwalls of Schell and Gonzalez. Further back, Gordinis and various British specials swelled the field.

The Vanwalls - three this time - did not make an impression in this race after a good start by Schell but from the third row Brooks made excellent progress to join BRM teammate Hawthorn at the front of the field. Fangio came through to split the home heros only to spin, then Moss fought his way through to the front.

The BRM challenge subsequently fizzled out, leaving Moss and the still impressive Salvadori ahead of Fangio. Alas, Salvadori's fuel tank retaining strap broke, then his engine failed. Moss also found trouble, in the form of an ignition fault which handed Fangio the lead. It then transpired that Moss had started on a part fuel load and replenishment set him further back. Soon afterwards gearbox failure cost all hope. That left Fangio and Collins first and second, ahead of Behra (who had been lapped by Moss) while Perdisa finished seventh. Pole man Moss had the consolation of fastest race lap.

Nurburgring (D) August 5
German Grand Prix
Moss 2   (Q: 4)
Behra 3   (Q: 8)
Maglioli .... NR   (Q: 7)

The improving British teams avoided the tortuous Nurburgring. Maserati fielded

Diary continues on page 70

1956 was the year of aerodynamic experiments. At Francorchamps the works cars appeared with ducted radiators, as seen here in testing at Monza. Later in the year Monza saw the 'offset' cars debut in the Grand Prix. The offset machine with its prop shaft running alongside the driver's seat is pictured overleaf.

overthrow the Italians.

The Maserati performance bounced back at Silverstone, Moss claiming pole and the moral victor. He was let down by an ignition fault, subsequently a gearbox failure. At the 'Ring Fangio had a slight edge while the Monza finale looked as though it was going to be hopeless for Maserati in the light of the lack of straightline speed that had been evident at Francorchamps and Rheims. However, new lower drag 'offset' cars developed by Alfieri tipped the balance and Moss won while the faster D.50s again grappled with tyre problems.

Alfieri's experiments in drag reduction started Francorchamps with all the team cars featuring long tapering nose cowls with the radiator mounted further forward, a smaller inlet duct and a top duct to exhaust the hot air from the radiator. Chassis 2501 was further modified with high cockpit sides and a full wrap around screen, following Vanwall practice. This car was raced by Moss both at Francorchamps and Rheims. At Rheims Maserati also produced the '55 stream-liner - 2518 - equipped with disc brakes. The brakes had to run without a servo due to the use

Moss in the low drag car supported by Behra and Umberto Maglioli, who stood in when Perdisa injured himself during a supporting race. The field comprised Maserati, Ferrari's modified Lancias, Maserati privateers and a couple of slow Gordinis. In practice only Maranello's finest got around the daunting 14 mile circuit in under ten minutes: Fangio, Collins and Castellotti. Fourth fastest, Moss lost almost a second a mile to Fangio.

Fangio took command on the first lap, chased by Collins while Castellotti had a time wasting incident with Moss. Moss escaped unscathed and gave chase but there was no way he could catch Fangio and Collins, in spite of a lap record breaking effort. Collins suffered a split fuel tank while Fangio replied to Moss' challenge with another lap record and was the worthy victor. All four other modified Lancias broke and Behra finished third while (a victim of steering failure) Maglioli retired (as did Salvadori who again had the Gilby car flying).

Monza (I) September 2
Italian Grand Prix
Moss................ 1 *(Q: 6)*
Behra ....NR *(Q: 5)*
Maglioli .... NR *(Q:12) (Behra)*
Villoresi.......... NR *(Q: 8)*

For the Monza high speed blind Maserati built two special low line offset seat cars for Moss and Behra, leaving Maglioli and Villoresi in regular machines. Held over Monza Park's combined road and banked course, this was the World Championship finale. Fangio led the title chase but both Behra and Collins could overhaul him given a win plus the point for fastest lap. Ferrari countered with six cars, as usual modified D.50s while Vanwall

pitched in with three cars. A mixed bag of private 250Fs, Gordini and Connaughts filled out the entry.

The Ferrari Lancias were quickest in practice, in spite of tyre troubles reminiscent of the previous year. The grid formed up as Fangio, Castellotti, Musso with Taruffi's Vanwall ahead of Behra and Moss. In the race Castellotti and Musso tried going flat out only to suffer shredded treads: the race was left as Moss versus Fangio and Collins and Schell in the fastest of three Vanwalls, Taruffi and Behra next up.

Taruffi was soon in the pits but Schell was able to relieve Moss of the lead temporarily. Then Fangio took a turn at leading, the three leaders very close. Behra held fourth, Collins falling back with tyre trouble. Musso came back into the picture catching and passing Behra then Fangio fell back with broken steering leaving Schell to battle Moss. Behra also met trouble, and he took over Maglioli's car only to suffer another breakage while Villoresi also fell out.

Schell had started on a half tank. Moss overtook him during a short shower and the Vanwall retired soon after refuelling. Moss looked all set to win only to run out of fuel near the end. Piotti was able to use his private 250F to shunt the stranded offset car to the pits and Moss rejoined second to Musso's Ferrari. This time luck was in Moss' favour: Musso suffered broken steering and crashed out.

Moss finished six seconds ahead of Fangio who had been handed Collins' car and had made up lost ground in magnificent style. Collins' sporting gesture let the Argentinian retain the World Championship with three points over Moss.

Melbourne (AUS) December 2
Australian Grand Prix
Moss 1
Behra 2

There was no factory opposition and Moss won easily, beating Behra who used a 300S 3.0 litre sports car engine.

of a five speed gearbox and since pedal pressure was uncomfortably high the car was not raced. After Rheims the streamliner was destroyed in a factory fire.

With the Francorchamps-type nose Alfieri tried both top and bottom ducting for the radiator air exit but after Rheims Maserati reverted to standard 250F bodywork, though Moss ran 2501 as a low drag special once again, at the 'Ring. At Silverstone top speeds were measured on the Hanger Straight and fastest of all was the diminutive BRM of Hawthorn at 137.40m.p.h. followed by Schell's Vanwall at 136.8m.p.h. and Brooks' BRM at 136.36m.p.h. None of the Italian cars exceeded 135m.p.h, Fangio recording 134.83m.p.h. Collins 134.33m.p.h. and Moss the quickest Maserati speed of 133.83m.p.h.

Since Rheims Alfieri had been working on the radical new chassis with an offset prop shaft to enable the driver to sit lower in the car, primarily to the benefit of aerodynamic drag. The aims of the so called offset version were to lower the frontal area and to lower the centre of gravity. The frame was only slightly modified with a 20mm. longer wheelbase though the use of thinner wall tubing made it a little lighter. The suspension was unchanged while the engine was angled five degrees in Lancia D.50 fashion to throw the prop shaft towards the left rear corner. The five speed gearbox was duly redesigned with the bevel input shifted to the left rather than on the centre line of the car.

The new transmission arrangement allowed

Front view of the Monza offset car, bonnet off revealing how the engine is angled to throw the prop shaft to the left of the driver. The cockpit is no longer symmetical, as is also evident on the previous page.

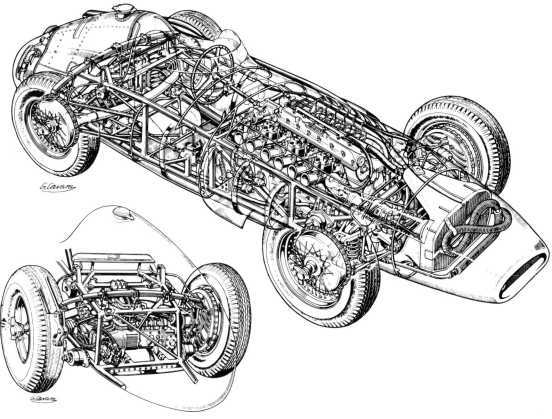

Details from 1956. The top photograph shows the 10mm. plug engine, which had a revised combustion chamber. The centre photograph shows an injected engine, converted motorcycle carburettors providing the slide throttles. The throttle linkage is connected to the pump which is concealed under the exhaust manifold. The lower photograph is a rear suspension detail.

the seat to be set alongside the prop shaft, the 'shaft then passing beneath the driver's left knee while the cockpit was off-centre, the car no longer symmetical about its longitudinal axis. The prop shaft ran alongside a seat set approximately 200mm. lower than standard. The steering box was relocated on the main crossmember behind the engine - there free from engine vibration - and the line of the steering column and the bonnet were lowered. A new fuel tank formed a faired head rest and was mounted on rubber blocks and was secured by spring-loaded bolts.

The nose was longer and tapering and the body was generally lower and sleeker. The offset car was much lower than the Vanwall, its inspiration. It approached the question of drag reduction from the point of view of frontal area rather than the overall form, drag being the product of a non dimensional drag co-efficent (very low for the Vanwall) and frontal area. Two versions of the offset 250F were built, one each for Moss and Behra.

The offset car ran a little higher than the standard machine, hopefully to improve underbody airflow. This had the advantage that the tail did not scrape on the banking, unlike the regular cars. At one stage Piotti's tail fairing was completely wiped off. The fact that Moss ran out of fuel was later traced to a fuel tank leak, but in any case with Piotti's help he won. Nevertheless, Alfieri decided to drop the offset project, having a complete rethink for '57 which involved the introduction of a V12 engine.

The offset car was a radical answer to the problem of an ageing design running out of development potential. Prior to the ambitious project Alfieri had concentrated his efforts upon disc braking and fuel injection, with far less success. The only time discs were publicly aired was at Rheims on the streamliner, which also ran an injection engine. The main problem with disc brake development was the distance between Modena and the brake manufacturers. Since no great advantage was evident this technical path was not pursued avidly. Injection engines appeared more frequently in 1956, first in the works car lent to Moss for the Easter Monday Goodwood International.

The Goodwood car carried an indirect injection system based on an OM/Bosch pump. The

six plunger pump was mounted to the left of the engine, under the exhaust manifolds and was driven via an external triple roller chain from a spiral gear taking power off the vertical magneto drive shaft that side. Plunger movement was controlled in accordance with throttle slide position rather than an inlet pressure sensor, via a mechanical linkage. An adapted motorcycle carburettor body provided a slide for each inlet tract and the injector nozzle was positioned within the body just below the throttle.

The indirect injection engine offered a higher top end power but the pick up was poor and the power came in with too much of a rush and Moss' old private car on carburettors was just about as quick as the new machine. Nevertheless, Moss won the weakly supported Richmond Trophy race with the experimental device.

The indirect injection engine was subsequently used by Behra at Syracuse, then appeared in the spare car at Monte Carlo. The next development was a direct injection engine which was on hand for the spare car in Monaco and was used in the spare car at Francorchamps, then the Rheims streamliner. This engine proved more civilised but was heavy on fuel and thus was not raced. After Rheims the team abandoned fuel injection experiments which were proving very time consuming and were not paying dividends. Alfieri turned his attention instead to the offset cars.

Early on the team had lost Menditeguy due to a sports car accident, and the growing sports car programme was a greater drain than ever. From Monaco onwards the Formula One team shrank from four to three regular cars. Nevertheless, six new works cars were phased in during the season, including the two offset machines. In addition, two cars were constructed for customers: 2519 was for Luigi Piotti while 2524 went to Francesco Godia-Sales. Meanwhile, a number of '54/'55 factory cars were disposed of: 2511 was sold to the Italian Scuderia Centro-Sud, 2514 to Horace Gould, 2515 to Scuderia Guastalla, 2516 to Reg Hunt.

Of the new works cars, the standard machines were 2520 - 2523, the offset cars 2525 for Moss, 2526 for Behra. Chassis 2523 appeared in April based on the frame from 2507, the Gilby Engineering car which had been shunted at Oulton Park in '54. Gilby had been supplied a new frame and this year the old one was taken from the dump and was straightened to produce a 'muletto' for the factory team. However, later 2523 was apparently rebuilt around a new frame and in this form it went to the Australian Grand Prix. With so many cars in existence chassis numbers were getting a little muddled. Of course, the number counted for nothing when it came to the business of winning races. And in that business the 250F was still very effective.

Stirling Moss in action at the Nurburgring in '56 in the 'low drag' car first seen at Spa Francorchamps. He could not beat Fangio this weekend but took a good second place.

Welcome Back

There were important changes to the 1957 Maserati World Championship challenge. The three year old 250F design was revamped, a new V12 engine was developed and the racing department was re-organised. The revamp followed the lead of the '56 Monza offset car with its lower frontal area, the target lower drag. The angled engine and transmission package was not carried forward but the general lines of the '57 body followed those of the Vanwall inspired Monza machine: it was thus lower and sleeker, with high cockpit sides and a head fairing formed by the fuel tank.

Another major change was the frame - a new stiffer structure of smaller diameter tubing and increased triangulation was introduced, primarily to save weight. The brakes were wider still, with the cooling fins offset from the hubs in the airstream. Otherwise the mechanicals were familiar, the emphasis on development of the new V12 machine, while the trumpets of the Weber carburettors were enclosed in a sealed aluminium box fed air by a prominent tubular intake on the bonnet. The aim was to impart a degree of pressurisation to the incoming charge air.

The twelve cylinder project had commenced in '56 as a radical new package based around a flat 12 engine, though still following the established 250F layout. However, time and money ran short and the new engine was changed to a 60 degree V12 to fit the existing chassis. The plan was that the so called 250F T2 should phase out the revamped six cylinder 'lightweights' during the course of the season.

Meanwhile, the racing 'shop was clearly divided between works car preparation, experimental work and customer support. No further customer cars were built but existing privateers were sufficiently numerous to keep things very

busy in the Viale Ciro Menotti and customer demands had distracted attention from the factory team effort in '56. Further, the sports car racing team continued to extend its ambitions so that was another sap on resources.

Stirling Moss relinquished the post of Team Leader to join the ever improving Vanwall effort but Fangio had been dissatisfied at Ferrari in the light of which Maserati were delighted to be able to welcome him back into the fold at long last. However, he would not commit his signature to a Maserati contract until he had tried the lightweight in Argentina...

Should it come to that, Behra was happier to play number two to Fangio than he had been serving under Moss and the enthusiastic Harry Schell was invited to join the team, moving over from Vanwall, while Menditeguy rejoined. Moss' new Vanwall could not be readied until the start of the European season so the departing Englishman bolstered the team in Argentina. In addition to three revamped lightweights Maserati prepared an old style 'muletto' - actually chassis 2501 - on which to try out new ideas and with additionally V12 cars to test Scarlatti was marked down as reserve driver.

250F leads Vanwall at Monza in 1957. Stirling Moss moved to the Vanwall team for 1957 as it emerged as a real force to be reckoned with.

DIARY

Buenos Aires (ARG) January 13
Argentinian Grand Prix

Fangio	1	(Q: 2)
Moss	8	(Q: 1)
Behra	2	(Q: 3)
Menditeguy	3	(Q: 8)

The 1957 specification lightweight 250F was ready for the Argentinian Grand Prix at Buenos Aires on January 13: a trio of cars for Fangio, Moss and Behra while Menditeguy drove an old-style 'muletto'. Ferrari comprised the opposition, fielding six yet further modified Lancia-Ferraris (Castellotti, Collins, Hawthorn, Musso, Perdisa, Gonzalez). Ferrari used nitromethane for extra power during practising yet the Maseratis were faster with Moss, Fangio and Behra heading the grid.

Poleman Moss was unlucky enough to suffer a broken throttle linkage on the first lap leaving Behra and Fangio to chase the fast starting Castellotti. Moss lost eight laps and meanwhile Behra assumed the lead and Collins came through to second. Castellotti spun back a few more places then Collins took Behra for the lead but around the one hour mark Fangio emerged ahead. Collins clutch had failed and on the same lap Fangio had overtaken Behra.

Hawthorn also lost his clutch, this promoting Menditeguy to fourth behind Castellotti who could not keep the leading 250Fs in sight. Eventually Castellotti lost a wheel leaving a clean sweep for Maserati, with Harry Schell's Centro Sud 250F in fourth place. Centro Sud was heavily supported by the factory this season. Moss finished eighth, seven laps down with fastest lap to his credit. The best Ferrari could manage was fifth for the Gonzalez car.

Buenos Aires (AGR) January 27
Buenos Aires Grand Prix

Fangio	1
Moss	NR
Behra	2
Menditeguy	6 (Moss)

Two weeks later the Buenos Aires Autodrome was baking: it was hotter than for the '55 Argentinian Grand Prix but at least this race was run over two heats. Fangio and Moss tied for fastest time in practice and Fangio took pole but again Castellotti made the best start. Collins was second but was soon overcome by the heat, then Moss took the lead only to suffer likewise. Nevertheless, Fangio and Behra finished first and second for Maserati with Castellotti, Hawthorn and Musso ahead of Menditeguy.

Castellotti rocketed off again in the second heat only to spin, leaving Hawthorn ahead of Fangio and Behra. The heat got to the Ferrari driver towards the end and Behra came through, ahead of Fangio. However, having taken over Musso's car Collins carved through to win, with Fangio third suffering a broken exhaust and Hawthorn fourth. Moss took over Menditeguy's car but it was out of the running. Fangio won on aggregate times, from Behra and Collins/Musso.

Syracuse (I) April 7
Syracuse Grand Prix

Behra	NR
Schell	NR
Scarlatti	DNS

Maserati faced Ferrari and Vanwall in the Sicilian non-championship European season opener, with Connaught in for good measure. Moss had defected to Vanwall, where he joined Brooks. Ferrari likewise ran two works cars, for Collins and Musso. Behra was out in a lightweight 250F, Schell in the muletto while Giorgio Scarlatti was assigned V12 test driver. Both Schell and Scarlatti tried the V12 car but it was not a success and was withdrawn from the race.

The grid order was Collins, Musso, Moss, Brooks, Behra, Schell. Behra's car started overheating just before the start: he swapped with Schell who retired the sick machine after just two laps with a seized water pump. Alas, the older car had a broken frame and Behra also fell by the wayside. Meanwhile, Moss showed the Vanwall was now a real third force by leading convincingly while Brooks came through to second, only for his engine to fail. Eventually a split injection pipe on Moss' car left victory to the '57 specification Lancia-Ferrari of Collins.

Pau (F) April 22
Pau Grand Prix

Behra	1
Schell	2

Neither Ferrari nor Vanwall attended the Pau Grand Prix on Easter Monday and Behra's works 250F won the street race at a canter, a works Connaught taking third.

Monte Carlo (MON) May 19
Monaco Grand Prix

Fangio	1	(Q: 1)
Menditeguy	NR	(Q: 6)
Schell	NR	(Q: 8)
Scarlatti	NR	(Q:14) (Schell)

The first European round of the World Championship brought 250F lightweights for Fangio, Menditeguy and Schell (Behra had suffered injuries practising for the Mille Miglia) while Herrmann and Scarlatti shared the muletto. The V12 machine was again aired unconvincingly and was not raced. Ferrari had cars for Collins, Hawthorn, Musso, Wolfgang von Trips and Trintignant (Castellotti had been killed in a testing accident) while Vanwall entered Moss and Brooks. BRM, Connaught and Cooper were also represented, Brabham's strange looking mid engine Climax-Cooper Formula Two car having grown to 2.2 litres.

Diary continues on page 80

Drifting Home

The Maserati 250F lightweight was good enough to win yet another World Championship for Fangio in the face of stiff opposition, from Ferrari and in particular from Moss with the Vanwall. The lightweight was not good enough to allow the Argentinian to dominate everywhere, as he had done with the W196 two years earlier. But it was effective on circuits as diverse as Monaco and Rouen.

Nevertheless, the lightweight only allowed Fangio to clearly stamp his authority at Buenos Aires - a race from which Vanwall was absent - and Rouen (which Moss missed through illness). At Rouen the combination of Fangio and the 250F was in its element, the car drifting through the fast, taxing downhill sweeps in a smoothly blended series of beautifully controlled four wheel drifts. It was a classic example of high speed car control by a Great driver in one of the best balanced front engined Grand Prix cars ever built.

Maserati, Vanwall and Ferrari were closely matched at Monaco while at Aintree Maserati and Vanwall played the leading roles. However, the Vanwall was at sea at the Nurburgring and here Ferrari fought Maserati. Then at Monza Ferrari was again out of the frame as Maserati and Vanwall vied for supremacy, Vanwall this time having an edge. Clearly, the great strength of the lightweight was its all round ability: nowhere was Fangio out of the picture. Fangio later remarked: "the lightweight 250F was nicely balanced, responsive, fast and suited my driving style".

In view of the lightweight's unstinting competitiveness the V12 project was an unnecessary distraction, the complex new machine lacking any advantage - even at Monza its tyre wear and fuel consumption was far too high for it to count. However, it was an important preparation for the future. Clearly, the four year old 250F design could not live for ever, especially with the threat of shorter races and hydrocarbon fuel looming. The V12 was a logical answer to the challenge of the future. Meantime, in 1957 the 250F was in its prime, so too was Fangio.

There was no significant car development over the course of the season, the lightweight model essentially right from the word go. In contrast the further modified D.50 was chopped and changed, another disappointment for Ferrari's talented engineers. Of course, the Maranello challenge had been weakened by Fangio's defection to Maserati. With Fangio and Moss in rival camps Ferrari was at a definite disadvantage.

Worse, the bigger bore engine developed for the new season (80mm. x 62mm. - a stroke: bore ratio of 0.775) did not appear to unleash stronger horses in spite of its higher r.p.m. potential. Further, chassis modifications - which included discarding the distinctive panniers altogether - lacked direction. Coil springs were introduced for the front suspension, and for an experimental swing axle rear suspension. That might have been forward thinking but there was also a regressive semi-ladder frame as all trace of Jano's adventurous 1954 concept vanished.

While Ferrari blew hot and cold and behind the scenes put much effort into an all new Jano V6 engine for 1958, Vanwall continued its strong progression into a serious Championship challenger, the green car working well at Monaco, Rouen, Aintree and Monza, only showing its youth at the 'Ring. The car was not radically changed from the promising '56 model but the team was learning all the time and in Moss it had a driver with the ability to ensure it a fully deserved front running status.

Vandervell put a tremendous effort into its '57

Fangio took pole from Collins and Moss, all three within a second. Moss' Vanwall led the start while Collins passed Fangio for second on the second lap and set after Moss, drawing away from the 250F. However, on the fourth lap Moss' brakes locked and he failed to negotiate the chicane scattering poles and sand-bags and knocking out his car and the pursuing Ferrari. The sister Ferrari of Hawthorn also became a victim of the melee while Brooks' Vanwall was able to reverse out to chase the one ace who dodged it all...

The order at the end of the fourth lap was Fangio, Brooks, Schell, von Trips, Menditeguy with Scarlatti running well back. Around quarter distance Schell's engine failed, while Menditeguy was now well back after an unscheduled stop. That left Brabham's Cooper fourth but Menditeguy recovered to pass it. Then Scarlatti handed over to Schell. Menditeguy climbed to third only for his car to retire around half distance, and all the while Fangio had the measure of Brooks who in turn was under no threat from von Trips.

Schell made progress only to find suspension trouble so only one factory 250F finished but it was in the lead. Trip's engine failed and at the end of a race of attrition Masten Gregory brought Centro Sud's works supported 250F home third, Brabham having suffered a broken fuel pump drive.

Rouen (F) July 7
French Grand Prix
Fangio .... 1 (Q: 1)
Behra .... 5 (Q: 2)
Schell .... 6 (Q: 4)
Menditeguy .... NR (Q: 9)

The gap in the World Championship calendar is explained by the Belgian and Dutch races succumbing to financial pressures. Thus, business resumed at Rouen Les Essarts in July. Maserati had lightweight cars for Fangio, Behra and Schell while Menditeguy had the muletto and there was also a modified V12 car with Scarlatti listed as driver, should it be deemed raceworthy. Again Ferrari had four Lancia-based machines with its Monaco line up but Vanwall had lost Moss and Brooks to sickness and injury respectively, substituting Salvadori and Lewis Evans. Cooper and BRM helped make up the numbers.

Musso made the front row but practice was dominated by Maserati, Fangio and Behra making the best times. The V12 car showed increased promise - Fangio setting second fastest time in it - but again was not raced.

Behra led from the start but Musso went into the lead on the first lap with Fangio third, Collins fourth and Schell fifth. On the next lap Fangio moved into second then after three laps he took the lead and drew away, to win handsomely. Collins passed Behra to give Ferrari second and third positions. Musso was second with a new lap record to his credit while Collins was third, having passed his Italian teammate only to fall back with gearbox bothers. Hawthorn was fourth, ahead of Behra and Schell both of whom suffered engine maladies, Behra having to push his oil starved car in. Menditeguy also suffered a broken engine, a legacy of an off-course excursion which ripped off oil lines.

Rheims (F) July 14
Rheims Grand Prix
Fangio .... NR
Behra 2
Schell 4
Menditeguy .... NR

A week on a non-championship race was held at Rheims, traditional home of the French Grand Prix. Two of the lightweights had gone back to the factory for fettling, leaving the Rouen winner which was driven by Schell. Fangio drove a '56 offset car, Behra the muletto. There were also two V12 cars, the Monte Carlo/ Rouen machine plus a newer example, this one based on the other '56 Monza offset car. Menditeguy tried these.

The engine quickly failed in the new V12 car but Menditeguy raced the original example. The principal opposition was as at Rouen and while Fangio was fastest in practice, Lewis Evans was second, lining up his Vanwall alongside Behra.

Lewis Evans was even more impressive in the race, leading until slowed by fading brakes and oil spraying onto his goggles. That gave the advantage, not to Fangio but to Musso who had the measure of the World Champion driving a Ferrari Lancia in original guise. The other Maranello runners had retired but there was no denying Musso victory. Fangio and Behra disputed second place until Fangio went off with locked brakes. Schell finished fourth behind the unlucky Lewis Evans while Menditeguy suffered a broken gearbox around half distance.

Aintree (GB) July 20
British Grand Prix
Fangio .... NR (Q: 4)
Behra .... NR (Q: 2)
Schell .... NR (Q: 7)
Menditeguy ..... NR (Q:11)

Back at Aintree, the British Grand Prix saw Fangio, Behra and Schell drive lightweights, Menditeguy the muletto. No sign of the V12 engine on this slow circuit. Vanwall fielded Moss, Brooks and Lewis Evans while Ferrari had its usual quartet and BRM and Cooper again added to the numbers. Sadly, the under-financed Connaught team had closed down.

Fangio was off-form leaving Behra to split Moss and Brooks on the grid. Behra made the best start but Moss led the early laps only to suffer an engine malady,

Diary continues on page 82

angio took a
omfortable victory for
Aaserati at Monte
Carlo in '57, three key
ompetitors crashing
ut on the fifth lap.

programme, to the extent of building sufficient cars not to have to race the same chassis twice in succession. Its improving machine was clothed in a slippery body designed by aerodynamic expert Frank Costin while its suspension design was the work of acknowledged expert Colin Chapman and its potent engine was derived

from the successful Norton motorcycle racing single. These promising elements were well blended by the maturing team.

The Vanwall had a well designed, notably stiff multi tubular frame with coil springs over tubular dampers at front and rear. The front suspension employed wishbones, the rear a de Dion

leaving Behra securely in first place. Moss took over Brooks' car - Brooks suffering a sore leg - and worked it up from ninth to third, all the while steadily gaining ground on Behra. Then the 250F's crankshaft broke, the second placed Ferrari of Hawthorn punctured a tyre on an engine fragment and Moss was left a not undeserving victor. Meanwhile, all the works Maseratis had failed. Mendiquy went first - prop shaft - then Schell - water pump - then Fangio - valve gear - finally Behra.

Nurburgring (D) August 4
German Grand Prix

Fangio	1	(Q: 1)
Behra	6	(Q: 3)
Schell	7	(Q: 6)
Scarlatti	10	(Q:13)

The German Grand Prix found Mendiquy replaced by Scarlatti, the Argentinian having returned home. Scarlatti drove the muletto alongside the regular lightweight trio, again no sign of the V12. Ferrari entered Hawthorn, Collins and Musso while Vanwall had its Aintree trio but the British car was at sea on its first trip to the 14 mile mountain circuit. Only three marques were represented but the Italian cars were closely matched, Fangio taking pole by less than three seconds from Hawthorn with Behra third and Collins fourth.

However, the 250F's tyre wear was higher, too high to run the race non-stop. That being the case, the Maserati team planned to start on half tanks and refuel during the tyre stop.

Hawthorn and Collins jumped into an immediate lead but by the end of lap three Fangio was ahead and starting to draw away. Persistently breaking the lap record, by the end of lap twelve the Maserati

was able to draw into the pits with around half a minute's advantage. Alas, the stop took the best part of a minute, not counting time lost decelerating then accelerating again: Fangio found himself over threequarters of a minute adrift.

Collins now took the lead, breaking Fangio's new record in passing Hawthorn. Meanwhile, Behra, who had made his stop two laps earlier from fourth place now lay seventh. At the end of this lap Schell stopped from fourth and resumed behind Behra.

Musso and Moss thus found themselves fourth and fifth, well behind Fangio. At first Fangio made no impression on the Ferraris ahead - thinking he was in trouble Ferrari signalled 'steady' at the end of lap 14. From the Maserati pit Bertocchi signalled 'flat out' and Fangio pulled back almost a second a mile on lap 15. The Ferrari pit was soon urging its men on, yet on lap 17 Fangio closed to within half a minute and on lap 18 he made the first ever 90m.p.h. lap of the Nurburgring, cutting the deficit to 20 seconds.

Hawthorn now led and by the end of lap 20, with two more to go, the flying Maserati was looming large in Collins' mirrors having lapped at close on 92m.p.h! Fangio had broken the lap record no less than ten times and nothing was going to deny him the triumph he so richly deserved, though Hawthorn fought him every inch of the way, finishing less than four seconds adrift. Collins was driving virtually one-eyed, a stone from Fangio's car having broken a goggle lens as the master passed by. Totally eclipsed, Behra finished sixth, Schell seventh, Scarlatti - who ran non stop - tenth.

Pescara (I) August 18
Pescara Grand Prix

Fangio	2	(Q: 1)
Behra	NR	(Q: 4)
Schell	3	(Q: 5)
Scarlatti	6	(Q:10)

Two weeks later Maserati presented the same drivers and equipment for the Pescara

Grand Prix over an even longer - 15.9 mile - mountain circuit composed of everyday roads. The Rheims V12 car was given another airing but was not nimble enough for the many sinuous parts of the course. Although the race had World Championship status Ferrari sent only one car, this loaned to Musso. Ferrari had a policy of not running on Italian road circuits. Vanwall ran its regular trio and a pair of Coopers completed the field.

Musso and Moss joined Fangio on the front row and the Ferrari led from the start, chased by Moss, Behra and Fangio. Brooks retired on the first lap while Schell and Scarlatti ran in midfield. Moss was very much on form and he dislodged Musso from the lead on the second lap while Fangio displaced Behra who retired with oil pipe breakage on the fourth lap. At that stage positions at the front were static while Schell soon found himself fourth, largely through the misfortunes of others.

Musso found his share of misfortune as the Ferrari engine failed but there was no denying Moss his win. He was even able to pit to check the cause of fluctuating oil pressure. Fangio ran home three minutes adrift after hitting a kerb and bending a wheel. Schell was third, Scarlatti sixth overcoming engine and clutch bothers.

Monza (I) September 8
Italian Grand Prix

Fangio	2	(Q: 4)	
Behra	NR	(Q: 5)	
Schell	NR	(Q: 6)	
Scarlatti	5	(Q:12)	(Schell)

Monza hosted the World Championship finale and Maserati was fearful of the speed of the Vanwalls on the fast road circuit employed this year. Consequently, Behra elected to race the V12 car, further developed if not yet fully sorted. Since the V12 challenge was still an unknown

Diary continues on page 84

tube located via a Watt's linkage. Braking was by Vandervell-Goodyear discs, inboard at the rear while the gearbox - integral with the final drive - was five speed with Porsche synchromesh.

The in line four aluminium alloy/ iron liner Vanwall engine had typically over-square dimensions of 96mm. x 86mm. - a stroke:bore ratio of 0.896 - and the usual hemispherical head with two valves at the relatively narrow angle of 60 degrees included. The valves were driven directly through bucket tappets via twin overhead camshafts powered by a gear train on the front end. The valves were closed, unusually, by hairpin springs. Two plugs per cylinder were ignited via magnetos and the engine employed Bosch indirect injection, a system well honed since 1955. Following the withdrawal of Daimler Benz, Bosch gave Vandervell maximum assistance.

Vanwall ran its punchy four to 7,400r.p.m. unleashing a claimed 270b.h.p. on nitromethane - no less than 14.59b.h.p. per litre per 1000r.p.m. Thus, the three key '57 contenders enjoyed similar power outputs from four, six and eight cylinder units, the Vanwall engineers squeezing out more performance per 1000r.p.m. with the aid of well developed fuel injection and excellent breathing. At 7,400r.p.m. the Vanwall's mean piston speed was a worryingly high 4165 feet per minute, the speed matched by the Maserati six at 8,500r.p.m.

By this stage the Modena six was capable of sustaining as much as 8,700r.p.m. for short periods without blowing apart. Indeed, after the race at Casablanca The Autocar reported that Behra's rev counter tell tale registered 8,000r.p.m, Fangio's 9,000r.p.m. and that of Schell no less than 10,500r.p.m. Behra had won the race and Fangio had set fastest lap passing a reluctant Schell, who must have counted himself lucky to have gone on to see the chequered flag...

On nitromethane these days the engine was giving a maximum of 270b.h.p. at 8,000r.p.m. - 13.50b.h.p. per litre per 1000r.p.m. The engine retained a wide power band and it was the combination of this and the natural oversteer of the chassis that allowed Fangio to perfect the art of four wheel drift. Front wheels given a touch of opposite lock, the Master could control the attitude of the well balanced car via the throttle.

Fangio at Rouen, overleaf: a study in the art of car control. A touch of opposite lock, the master balances the car with the throttle. A tendency towards oversteer and a wide power band allows this breathtaking four wheel drift technique.

While Fangio progressed the art of Grand Prix driving and took most of the Maserati glory, Behra won at Pau, Modena and Casablanca and provided solid support for his Team Leader. In contrast, Menditeguy did not impress this season and consequently was relegated to the muletto. Eventually he returned to Argentina leaving Scarlatti deservedly elevated in the pecking order.

Chassis 2501 was the 'muletto' throughout the season. With the arrival of the lightweights, chassis 2520, '21 and '22 were all sold off, going to Stan Jones, John du Puy and Centro Sud respectively. Following its trip to Australia chassis 2523 - the fourth and last of the conventional cars built for the '56 works team - appears to have been broken up, though its original ex-Gilby frame was reportedly straightened to form the basis of the first V12 car, which was given the 2523 plate.

As we have seen, 2524 had been the last conventional customer car, going to Godia-Sales in '56 and no new customer machines were produced this year. Moss' '56 offset car - 2525 - reappeared at Rheims while the sister car - 2526 - apparently formed the basis of the third V12 car, 2531, though this offset transmission equipped machine had a brand new frame. Chassis 2527, '28 and '29 were the three lightweights. The only other chassis built in 1957 was 2530, another V12 machine with conventional rather than offset transmission, like the prototype.

Regardless of transmission, the V12 car was known as the 250F T2 and it had an engine specifically designed for high revolutions. It was distinctly over-square with bore and stroke of 68.7mm. x 56.0mm. - a stroke:bore ratio of 0.815 - and could thereby scream to 10,900r.p.m. without entering the uncertain region of plus-4000 feet per minute mean piston speed.

The challenge was to run to a five figure speed while retaining control of the valves and ignition. Alfieri had earlier tried desmodromic valve gear without success. Inspired by the W196, desmodromic development continued behind the scenes and for the time being a traditional head was employed, with coil springs. However, the revolutions envisaged meant it was necessary to use coil rather than the traditional magneto ignition which could not be guaranteed reliable at high speed.

Diary Continued

Modena (I) September 22
Modena Grand Prix
Behra 1
Schell 3
Scarlatti 5

quantity, Fangio and Schell drove regular lightweights while Scarlatti had the muletto. Vanwall replied with its regular trio while Ferrari again fielded four cars. Surprisingly Lewis Evans clinched pole, seven tenths faster than Fangio who was out-qualified by all three Vanwalls. The organisers ensured the front row was four cars wide so as to have the Red on it! Behra was a commendable fifth fastest in the V12 machine. Schell was next, ahead of Collins in the fastest Ferrari.

Musso made a tremendous start from the third row to split the Vanwall trio but at the end of the first lap it was Behra among the green cars in second place, Musso fifth ahead of Collins and Fangio. On the fourth lap Behra managed to dislodge Moss and Fangio moved up. Behra, Fangio and the three Vanwalls were now playing leapfrog in a slip-streaming, car taxing bunch while Schell led the Ferraris. Fangio led a number of laps, then each of the Vanwalls in turn headed the group, the British cars apparantly having an edge over Fangio and the V12 machine. Brooks was the first to wilt, with a jammed throttle, then Lewis Evans suffered stiff steering.

It then transpired that Behra had been playing hare: he needed fresh tyres and additional fuel. That left Fangio shadowing Moss and gradually slipping away while only Schell and Collins were still on the lead lap. Fangio dropped a lap behind after a stop for tyres and though Moss also pitted for rubber the Vanwall finished over 40 seconds ahead. Meanwhile, the V12 engine had overheated and Schell had suffered an oil leak. Schell took over Scarlatti's car but could not better fifth. Although Fangio was soundly beaten by Moss, second place was sufficient to secure him another World Championship title.

Although the title chase was over there were still two non-championship events to round out the year. The Modena Grand Prix was held over the autodrome used by both Maserati and Ferrari for testing. Maserati ran lightweights for Behra and Schell and the muletto for Scarlatti while the Monza V12 car was tried once more, to no avail. Ferrari provided the only serious opposition with enlarged - 1860 cc. - Dino V6 Formula Two cars for Musso and Collins. The race was held in two heats and during the first Musso pressed winner Behra extremely hard. The order in both heats was Behra, Musso, Schell, Collins, Scarlatti, Collins pushing Schell very hard in the second heat.

Casablanca (MOR) October 27
Moroccan Grand Prix
Fangio 4
Behra 1
Schell 5
Scarlatti 7

Encouraged by Modena, Ferrari entered 2.2 and 2.4 litre Dinos for Hawthorn and Collins respectively, both running on Avgas in anticipation of '58 regulations. A new circuit for this non-championship race found Maserati fielding lightweights for Fangio, Behra and Schell plus the usual muletto for Scarlatti and again testing the V12 without racing it. Vanwall lost Moss to Asian 'flu.

Brooks, Behra and Lewis Evans headed the grid but Collins' Ferrari with its light fuel load took the lead on the first lap. Feeling unwell, he soon spun to second behind Behra, started catching the 250F but went off. That left Fangio second but, also unwell, he spun and pitted, finishing fourth.

As usual, twin plugs were deemed essential, each with its own coil given the high rate of sparks required. Thus, there were 24 individual motorcycle-type Marelli ignition coils charged via two adapted magnetos. A twelve-point distributor was mounted on the back of each inlet camshaft, each distributor looking after one set of plugs. Electrical leads ran everywhere. Such unavoidable complexity could but add to the development headaches.

The engine was a 60 degree V12 and naturally was designed to run as a pair of six cylinder engines sharing a common crankshaft while the head was familiar and had twin overhead camshafts. The engine was, of course, of monobloc construction with detachable heads and wet iron liners were pressed into the alloy block. Again the engine was gear driven from the front of the crankshaft with the water, oil and fuel pumps also gear driven from the front power take-off.

The overall width of the engine and its narrow vee angle left little space for the induction system inside or out so Alfieri plumped for a vertical inlet port, the ports emerging between the two overhead camshafts. This provided a beneficial straight feed together with the possibility for a properly tuned intake system. Carburettors were employed following the failure of the injection programme.

Three Weber downdraught 35IDM doublechoke carburettors on each bank soon replaced the Solex items first tried. Early on an impressive 315b.h.p. was claimed at 10,000 on the test bed running four short exhausts with megaphones, this representing 12.6b.h.p. per litre per 1000r.p.m. However, the power band was extremely narrow.

As we have noted, chassis 2523 was adapted to produce the prototype 250F T2. Wider '57 drums were fitted. The major conversion was the steering system since it was no longer possible to run a drag link alongside the engine. Instead, a new steering box was mounted behind the radiator on a tubular structure and the steering column passed down the vee of the engine.

A larger radiator was specified to serve the V12 and the nose cowling was enlarged to accommodate this. Other distinguishing features were twin air intakes and (sometimes) two long (three into one) pipes discharging each side of the cockpit as different exhaust systems were evaluated. The dry weight was reportedly 650kg.

After the first appearance of T2-2523 at Syracuse, the exhaust pipes were shortened and were fitted with megaphone ends - reputedly unleashing higher power - while a modified five speed gearbox was installed. This had been tested on a V12 sports car driven by Herrmann in the Mille Miglia and was intended to allow all five gears to be fully utilised, rather than having first for starting only.

Nevertheless, the car again proved a handful on its second appearance at Monaco thanks to its narrow power band. It was necessary to scrabble around the numerous tight turns, freewheeling with the clutch out to keep the revs high enough to avoid an embarrassing lack of acceleration. Only Fangio was able to master the difficult machine well enough to record respectable lap times.

After Monaco the same chassis appeared fitted with a 3.5 litre sports car V12 and Indy Car-type wheels and tyres for the Monza 500 mile Formula One versus Indy Car race but poor handling caused by the unusual footwear led to its withdrawal.

The second T2 appeared at Rouen, 2530 with its lightweight-style chassis. Spur gears behind the clutch allowed the prop shaft to be lowered and to run at reduced speed. This T2 was characterised by a headrest fairing, a long tapering nose cowling and sunken NACA-type air ducts ahead of bonnet bulges over the inlet stacks. Underneath the bonnet, a large tray covered the engine to deflect the heat and leave the trumpets in cold air.

The power band of the engine had apparently been widened and Fangio, Schell and Menditeguy all drove the car, Fangio recording second fastest practice time in it. However, as he had recorded fastest in his six cylinder car he was not inclined to switch. Although more in its element at Rouen, again the T2 was not raced.

The third T2 was wheeled out at Rheims, this chassis 2531 which had an offset transmission.

It was accompanied by the prototype T2, which was the car Menditeguy raced to good effect after stalling at the start. Alas, he burned a piston, a fate shared by the newer car that had originally been intended for him to race. However, Maserati had managed to achieve a high level of dependability running on the bench.

Following Rheims, 2531 was used for testing at the sinuous Imola circuit where it ran back to back with a six-cylinder car. Now fitted with longer tuned megaphones, power was claimed as a honest sounding 310b.h.p. at 9,300r.p.m. - 13.33b.h.p. per litre per 1000r.p.m. The peak power speed had fallen as Alfieri sought a more civilised engine. Nevertheless, Fangio lapped a couple of seconds faster in the regular car.

Chassis 2531 was the V12 car seen at Pescara and was again the T2 representative at Monza. Since Imola it had been fitted with a revised exhaust system, each bank merging into a single tail pipe that swept over the rear wheels. This system dropped peak power but, significantly, widened the power band a little.

For Monza the engine was fitted with 14mm. plugs that gave better results than the original 10mm. items while a horizontal baffle in the nose intake allowed the driver to direct more air to the water or oil radiator, as required. The steering system was also slightly modified. Although a handful, the T2 was well suited to the high speed Monza circuit, as is evidenced by Behra's second row grid position. Alas, after running strongly in the race it over-heated.

At Modena the same car was seen with a larger radiator and header tank. It practised with alternative exhaust systems but again was not raced, as was once more the case in Morocco. Maserati could not overcome the handicap of a narrow power band in the time available and thus the T2 model did not show its full potential.

Although the V12 engine did not shine in '57 it promised to be the heart of a competitive '58 car, once its power characteristics had been completely tamed. With 130 octane Avgas becoming compulsory combustion chamber temperatures were set to increase since methanol had acted as a valuable internal coolant. This put the emphasis upon smaller cylinders.

The relatively small bore of the 12 cylinder engine offered the important advantage of a shorter heat path from the centre of the piston out to the liner wall. Further, by pushing the chemist out of the Formula One engine development 'shop the new fuel regulations put the spotlight firmly upon the mechanical engineer and his quest for ever increasing revolutions.

Alas, the potential of the V12 on Avgas would not be put to the test...

The cost of the T2 project in '57 was one of a number of factors that forced the closure of the Maserati racing team right at the end of the '57 season. Another factor was the ill fated sports car racing programme. Throughout the Fifties this had grown steadily, culminating in the hugely ambitious 4.5 litre V8-engined 450S of '56/'57.

This car, too powerful for the Maserati dynomometer, was dogged by bad luck and did not achieve success to match its awesome performance. Nevertheless, Maserati went to the final round of the '57 World Sports Car Championship at Caracas in Venezuela with a chance of taking the title. It came away with equipment too badly wrecked to sell off at the end of its very costly season.

The cost of the '57 Grand Prix and Sports Car programmes had been crippling and the fall of the Peron regime had made it extremely difficult to obtain settlement for some large invoices the company had raised following the sale of machine tools to Argentina. It all added up to a precarious financial situation and with the firm on the brink of bankruptcy the Italian government stepped in.

The government insisted that Maserati - still a viable entity - operated under a 'Controlled Administration' whereby economies were forced upon it, certain marketable assets were disposed of and debts were collected, while creditors were unable to seize the company's assets.

One condition of the Controlled Administration was that there was to be no further works racing programme, the company maintaining only its profitable customer racing service department. It was the end of an era.

The photographs on the next eight pages show scenes from the 250F's final, triumphant year of 1957. Depicted - in order - are Schell at Rouen in the V12 model (left), Behra at Rouen, Schell at Pescara, Schell at Monaco once again in a V12 car and Scarlatti at Monza.

P.S.

Maserati's most important customer for 1958 was Fangio who planned only a limited programme of races. Fangio's manager hired two '57 lightweights for the Argentinian races at the start of the '58 season and these were adapted to run on Avgas with modifications to carburation and a lower compression ratio. Fangio finished fourth in the Argentinian Grand Prix then won the Formula Libre Buenos Aires Grand Prix. Six days later, on February 8, privateer Ross Jensen took the last ever International race win for the model, the Invercargill Trophy race at Teretonga Park in New Zealand.

Another customer was American enthusiast Temple Buell who proposed running a pair of works fettled cars in '58, and he was prepared to finance further development. Further development of the costly V12 project was out of the question but the six cylinder 250F had a sound chassis and Alfieri had some ideas for improvement. With the advent of shorter races and lighter fuel loads Alfieri produced a lighter, more compact version dubbed the 'Piccolo'.

The Piccolo had a 40mm. shorter wheelbase, a lighter, more sophisticated tubular frame, a slimmed down gearbox and a smaller fuel tank. Around 75kg. was trimmed from the dry weight. Following testing at Modena, the prototype - chassis 2532 - made a brief appearance in practice for the Belgian Grand Prix in the hands of Buell's driver Masten Gregory, then both Gregory and Moss tried it at the Nurburgring.

Buell entered the car for the French Grand Prix, to be driven by Fangio. Fangio was now 47 years old and was having an unhappy year, during the course of which he had been kidnapped in Cuba. The French Grand Prix was his first World Championship race in Europe The clutch failed after 15 laps while he was battling for second place and at that point he made the decision to retire.

Maserati knew that it was effectively the end of the road for the 250F, too. Buell was subsequently supplied with two replicas of the Rheims car, chassis 2533 and 2534, the last of the 250F series, but without a top line driver his team was not a serious contender.

During '58 Alfieri planned an even more compact version of the 250F and when Colotti left to start his own design studio - Studio Tecnica Meccanica - he was able to take his drawings with him, together with a part completed car, which would have become chassis 2535. Instead it became the 'Tec-Mec' with the aid of American finance. Alas, there was no money for serious development, no major driver and the car only ever contested the '59 United States Grand Prix at Sebring, with an indifferent driver and without success.

Meanwhile, the 250F continued in service as a privateer machine, gradually diminishing in competitiveness as a new breed of Grand Prix car gathered speed. The 250F gained the dubious distinction of living from the very start to the very end of the 2.5 litre formula, one Bob Drake qualifying an example for the final race, the November 1960 United States Grand Prix.